Hispaania Maitsete Meistrid
Kirev Köögikunst Hispaania Moodi

Carmen Sánchez

CONTENT

- COD AJOARRIERO 25
  - INGREDIENTS 25
  - eMPLOYMENT 25
  - Lies 25
- steamed sherry 26
  - INGREDIENTS 26
  - eMPLOYMENT 26
  - Lies 26
- ALL OF PEBRE MONKFISH CREATES ME 27
  - INGREDIENTS 27
  - eMPLOYMENT 28
  - Lies 28
- SHAVED STITCH 29
  - INGREDIENTS 29
  - eMPLOYMENT 29
  - Lies 29
- NAVY CLAMS 30
  - INGREDIENTS 30
  - eMPLOYMENT 30
  - Lies 31
- MELUX WITH PEPPER 32
  - INGREDIENTS 32
  - eMPLOYMENT 32
  - Lies 32

CHICKEN DAPOLE WITH EVERYTHING 33
- INGREDIENTS 33
- eMPLOYMENT 33
- Lies 34

ROASTED DUCK 35
- INGREDIENTS 35
- eMPLOYMENT 35
- Lies 36

CHICKEN BODY VILLAROY 37
- INGREDIENTS 37
- eMPLOYMENT 37
- Lies 38

CHICKEN CROWN WITH LEMON MUSTARD SAUCE 39
- INGREDIENTS 39
- eMPLOYMENT 39
- Lies 40

PINTADA PROVIDED WITH CUMBLES AND MUSHROOMS 41
- INGREDIENTS 41
- eMPLOYMENT 41
- Lies 42

VILLAROY chicken breast stuffed with PIQUILLOS caramelized with MODENA vinegar 43
- INGREDIENTS 43
- eMPLOYMENT 43
- Lies 44

CHICKEN STUFFED WITH HAM, MUSHROOMS AND CHEESE 45

- INGREDIENTS 45
- eMPLOYMENT 45
- Lies 46

CHICKEN IN SWEET PLUM WINE 47
- INGREDIENTS 47
- eMPLOYMENT 47
- Lies 48

Orange chicken breast with cashew nuts 49
- INGREDIENTS 49
- eMPLOYMENT 49
- Lies 49

marinated partridge 50
- INGREDIENTS 50
- eMPLOYMENT 50
- Lies 50

COCKTAIL CHICKEN 51
- INGREDIENTS 51
- eMPLOYMENT 51
- Lies 52

COCA COLA style chicken wings 53
- INGREDIENTS 53
- eMPLOYMENT 53
- Lies 53

GARLIC CHICKEN 54
- INGREDIENTS 54
- eMPLOYMENT 54

- Lies 55
- CHICKEN CHILINDRÓN 56
  - INGREDIENTS 56
  - eMPLOYMENT 56
  - Lies 57
- pickled beans AND RED FRUITS 58
  - INGREDIENTS 58
  - eMPLOYMENT 58
  - Lies 59
- LEMON CHICKEN 60
  - INGREDIENTS 60
  - eMPLOYMENT 60
  - Lies 61
- CHICKEN SAN JACOBO WITH SERRANO COMPOUND, CASAR CAKE AND ROCKET 62
  - INGREDIENTS 62
  - eMPLOYMENT 62
  - Lies 62
- BREADED CHICKEN BACK 63
  - INGREDIENTS 63
  - eMPLOYMENT 63
  - Lies 63
- CHICKEN IN RED WINE 64
  - INGREDIENTS 64
  - eMPLOYMENT 64
  - Lies 65

BLACK BEER GRILLED CHICKEN 66
    INGREDIENTS 66
    eMPLOYMENT 66
    Lies 67
CHOCOLATE partridge 68
    INGREDIENTS 68
    eMPLOYMENT 68
    Lies 69
Calcutta Lark SERVED WITH RED FRUIT SAUCE 70
    INGREDIENTS 70
    eMPLOYMENT 70
    Lies 71
SAFE CHICKEN WITH PEACH SAUCE 72
    INGREDIENTS 72
    eMPLOYMENT 72
    Lies 73
CHICKEN FILLET STUFFED WITH SPINACH AND MOZARELA 74
    INGREDIENTS 74
    eMPLOYMENT 74
    Lies 74
INSURED CHICKEN WITH CAVA 75
    INGREDIENTS 75
    eMPLOYMENT 75
    Lies 75
CHICKEN WITH WALNUT SALUS 76
    INGREDIENTS 76

- eMPLOYMENT 76
- Lies 77

CHICKEN PEPTITOR 78
- INGREDIENTS 78
- eMPLOYMENT 78
- Lies 79

ORANGE CHICKEN 80
- INGREDIENTS 80
- eMPLOYMENT 80
- Lies 81

Chicken Stew WITH BERAGE 82
- INGREDIENTS 82
- eMPLOYMENT 82
- Lies 83

ROASTED CHICKEN WITH NUTS AND SOY 84
- INGREDIENTS 84
- eMPLOYMENT 84
- Lies 85

CHOCOLATE CHICKEN WITH ROASTED ALMONDS 86
- INGREDIENTS 86
- eMPLOYMENT 86
- Lies 87

LAMB KABS WITH PEPPERS AND PINEAPPLE VINEGAR 88
- INGREDIENTS 88
- eMPLOYMENT 88
- Lies 89

VICHI SMOKE FILLED IN PORT 90
    INGREDIENTS 90
    eMPLOYMENT 90
    Lies 91

MADRLEJA 92
    INGREDIENTS 92
    eMPLOYMENT 93
    Lies 93

CHOCOLATE WALNUT DOUBLE 94
    INGREDIENTS 94
    eMPLOYMENT 94
    Lies 95

CONFIT MEAT CAKE WITH SWEET WINE SAUCE 96
    INGREDIENTS 96
    eMPLOYMENT 96
    Lies 97

RABBIT WITH PUPPIES 98
    INGREDIENTS 98
    eMPLOYMENT 98
    Lies 99

MEAT BALLS IN PEPITORIA HAZELNUT SAUCE 100
    INGREDIENTS 100
    eMPLOYMENT 101
    Lies 101

MEAT STICKS WITH DARK BEER 102
    INGREDIENTS 102

eMPLOYMENT	102
Lies	103

TRIP TO MADRLEÑA 104
- INGREDIENTS 104
- eMPLOYMENT 104
- Lies 105

PORK'S FEET WITH APPLE AND MINT 106
- INGREDIENTS 106
- eMPLOYMENT 106
- Lies 107

CHICKEN BALLS WITH RASPBERRY SAUCE 108
- INGREDIENTS 108
- eMPLOYMENT 109
- Lies 109

stew with lamb 110
- INGREDIENTS 110
- eMPLOYMENT 110
- Lies 111

LAPUR CIVET 112
- INGREDIENTS 112
- eMPLOYMENT 112
- Lies 113

RABBIT WITH PEPPER RADA 114
- INGREDIENTS 114
- eMPLOYMENT 114
- Lies 114

CHEESE STUFFED CHICKEN POPULA WITH CURRY SAUCE 115
- INGREDIENTS 115
- eMPLOYMENT 116
- Lies 116

Page PIG IN RED WINE 117
- INGREDIENTS 117
- eMPLOYMENT 117
- Lies 118

COCHIFRITO NAVARRE 119
- INGREDIENTS 119
- eMPLOYMENT 119
- Lies 119

Beef Stew WITH PEANUT SAUCE 120
- INGREDIENTS 120
- eMPLOYMENT 120
- Lies 121

ROASTED PORK 122
- INGREDIENTS 122
- eMPLOYMENT 122
- Lies 122

CABBAGE INSURED 123
- INGREDIENTS 123
- eMPLOYMENT 123
- Lies 123

RABBIT COCKTAIL 124
- INGREDIENTS 124

- eMPLOYMENT 124
  - Lies 125
- ESCALOPE MADRILEÑA 126
  - INGREDIENTS 126
  - eMPLOYMENT 126
  - Lies 126
- GET RABBIT WITH MUSHROOMS 127
  - INGREDIENTS 127
  - eMPLOYMENT 127
  - Lies 128
- IBERIAN PORK RIBS WITH WHITE WINE AND HONEY 129
  - INGREDIENTS 129
  - eMPLOYMENT 129
  - Lies 129
- CHOCOLATE PEPPER PEARS 131
  - INGREDIENTS 131
  - eMPLOYMENT 131
  - Lies 131
- THREE CHOCOLATE CAKES WITH BISCUITS 132
  - INGREDIENTS 132
  - eMPLOYMENT 132
  - Lies 133
- MARING Switzerland 134
  - INGREDIENTS 134
  - eMPLOYMENT 134
  - Lies 134

HAZELNUT CREAM WITH BANANAS 135
    INGREDIENTS 135
    eMPLOYMENT 135
    Lies 136
LEMON CAKE WITH CHOCOLATE BASE 137
    INGREDIENTS 137
    eMPLOYMENT 137
    Lies 138
inquiry 139
    INGREDIENTS 139
    eMPLOYMENT 139
    Lies 140
INTXAURSALSA (walnut cream) 141
    INGREDIENTS 141
    eMPLOYMENT 141
    Lies 141
MERINGUE MILK 142
    INGREDIENTS 142
    eMPLOYMENT 142
    Lies 142
LANGUAGES OF THE MASS 143
    INGREDIENTS 143
    eMPLOYMENT 143
    Lies 143
ORANGE HATS 143
    INGREDIENTS 144

- eMPLOYMENT 144
- Lies 144

BAKED APPLE WITH PORT 145
- INGREDIENTS 145
- eMPLOYMENT 145
- Lies 145

COOKED MARINGO 146
- INGREDIENTS 146
- eMPLOYMENT 146
- Lies 146

KRAUTISHKA 147
- INGREDIENTS 147
- eMPLOYMENT 147
- Lies 147

KAMBLETA PEOPLE'S PANNA KOTA 147
- INGREDIENTS 148
- eMPLOYMENT 148
- Lies 148

AGRICULTURAL BISCUITS 149
- INGREDIENTS 149
- eMPLOYMENT 149
- Lies 150

MANGO PASTE 151
- INGREDIENTS 151
- eMPLOYMENT 151
- Lies 151

YOGURT CAKE	152
INGREDIENTS	152
eMPLOYMENT	152
Lies	152
BANANA COMPOST ROSEMARY	153
INGREDIENTS	153
eMPLOYMENT	153
Lies	153
GARDEN	154
INGREDIENTS	154
eMPLOYMENT	154
Lies	154
GYPSY HAND FOUNDED BY GRETIN	155
INGREDIENTS	155
eMPLOYMENT	155
Lies	155
FLANGE EGG	156
INGREDIENTS	156
eMPLOYMENT	156
Lies	156
JELLE CAVA WITH FLOWERS	157
INGREDIENTS	157
eMPLOYMENT	157
Lies	157
FRIES	158
INGREDIENTS	158

- eMPLOYMENT ... 158
  - Lies ... 158
- SAN JUAN COCA ... 159
  - INGREDIENTS ... 159
  - eMPLOYMENT ... 159
- Bolognese sauce ... 160
  - INGREDIENTS ... 160
  - eMPLOYMENT ... 160
  - Lies ... 161
- WHITE CHEESE (CHICKEN OR BEEF) ... 162
  - INGREDIENTS ... 162
  - eMPLOYMENT ... 162
  - Lies ... 162
- TOMATO CONSUL ... 164
  - INGREDIENTS ... 164
  - eMPLOYMENT ... 164
  - Lies ... 164
- ROBERT'S SAUCE ... 165
  - INGREDIENTS ... 165
  - eMPLOYMENT ... 165
  - Lies ... 165
- PINK sauce ... 166
  - INGREDIENTS ... 166
  - eMPLOYMENT ... 166
  - Lies ... 166
- FISH PROMOTION ... 167

- INGREDIENTS 167
- eMPLOYMENT 167
- Lies 167
- GERMAN SAUCE 168
  - INGREDIENTS 168
  - eMPLOYMENT 168
  - Lies 168
- Bold sauce 169
  - INGREDIENTS 169
  - eMPLOYMENT 169
  - Lies 170
- Dark Gravy (Chicken OR VIPI) 171
  - INGREDIENTS 171
  - eMPLOYMENT 171
  - Lies 172
- PICON MOJO 173
  - INGREDIENTS 173
  - eMPLOYMENT 173
  - Lies 173
- PESTO sauce 174
  - INGREDIENTS 174
  - eMPLOYMENT 174
  - Lies 174
- Sweet and sour sauce 175
  - INGREDIENTS 175
  - eMPLOYMENT 175

  Lies 175

GREEN MOJITO 176

  INGREDIENTS 176

  eMPLOYMENT 176

  Lies 176

BESAMEL sauce 177

  INGREDIENTS 177

  eMPLOYMENT 177

  Lies 177

Hunter's Sauce 178

  INGREDIENTS 178

  eMPLOYMENT 178

  Lies 178

AIOLI sauce 179

  INGREDIENTS 179

  eMPLOYMENT 179

  Lies 179

AMERICAN sauce 180

  INGREDIENTS 180

  eMPLOYMENT 180

  Lies 181

Dawn Sauce 182

  INGREDIENTS 182

  eMPLOYMENT 182

  Lies 182

BARBECUE SAUCE 183

- INGREDIENTS 183
- eMPLOYMENT 183
- Lies 184

BEARNAISE SAUCE 185
- INGREDIENTS 185
- eMPLOYMENT 185
- Lies 185

Carbonated sauce 187
- INGREDIENTS 187
- eMPLOYMENT 187
- Lies 187

CHARCUTERA sauce 188
- INGREDIENTS 188
- eMPLOYMENT 188
- Lies 188

CUMBERLAND SAUCE 189
- INGREDIENTS 189
- eMPLOYMENT 189
- Lies 190

KURRI sauce 191
- INGREDIENTS 191
- eMPLOYMENT 191
- Lies 192

Garlic sauce 193
- INGREDIENTS 193
- eMPLOYMENT 193

Lies	193
Grape sauce	194
INGREDIENTS	194
eMPLOYMENT	194
Lies	194
Cider sauce	195
INGREDIENTS	195
eMPLOYMENT	195
Lies	195
Ketchup	196
INGREDIENTS	196
eMPLOYMENT	196
Lies	197
PEDRO XIMENEZ wine sauce	198
INGREDIENTS	198
eMPLOYMENT	198
Lies	198
Cream sauce	199
INGREDIENTS	199
eMPLOYMENT	199
Lies	199
Mayonnaise sauce	200
INGREDIENTS	200
eMPLOYMENT	200
Lies	200
YOGURT AND SUSCE CAP	201

- INGREDIENTS 201
- eMPLOYMENT 201
- Lies 201

Devil's Sauce 202
- INGREDIENTS 202
- eMPLOYMENT 202
- Lies 202

SPANISH SAUCE 203
- INGREDIENTS 203
- eMPLOYMENT 203
- Lies 203

Hollandaise sauce 204
- INGREDIENTS 204
- eMPLOYMENT 204
- Lies 204

ITALIAN CLOTHES 205
- INGREDIENTS 205
- eMPLOYMENT 205
- Lies 205

Mousse sauce 207
- INGREDIENTS 207
- eMPLOYMENT 207
- Lies 207

RIMOULED sauce 208
- INGREDIENTS 208
- eMPLOYMENT 208

Lies	208
BIZCAINE SAUCE	209
INGREDIENTS	209
eMPLOYMENT	209
Lies	209
Red sauce	210
INGREDIENTS	210
eMPLOYMENT	210
Lies	210
BREAKFAST SAUCE	211
INGREDIENTS	211
eMPLOYMENT	211
Lies	211
ROMESCO sauce	212
INGREDIENTS	212
eMPLOYMENT	212
Lies	213
SOUBISE sauce	214
INGREDIENTS	214
eMPLOYMENT	214
Lies	214
TARTAR SAUCE	215
INGREDIENTS	215
eMPLOYMENT	215
Lies	215
Irish dressing	216

        INGREDIENTS 216
        eMPLOYMENT 216
        Lies 216
VEGETABLE SOUP 217
        INGREDIENTS 217
        eMPLOYMENT 217
        Lies 217

COD AJOARRIERO

INGREDIENTS

400 g crushed cod without salt

2 tablespoons of hydrated chorizo peppers

2 spoons of tomato sauce

1 green pepper

1 red pepper

1 clove of garlic

1 onion

1 chili pepper

Olive oil

Salt

eMPLOYMENT

Sauté and cook the vegetables over medium-low heat until soft. To the salt.

Add spoonfuls of chorizo pepper, tomato sauce and chili. Add the minced cod and cook for 2 minutes.

Lies

This is the perfect filling for a delicious empanada.

steamed sherry

INGREDIENTS

750 g of turkey

600 ml sherry wine

1 bay leaf

1 clove of garlic

1 lemon

2 tablespoons of olive oil

Salt

eMPLOYMENT

Cleanse your pain.

Add 2 tablespoons of oil to a hot pan and lightly fry the minced garlic.

Immediately add the crackers, wine, bay leaves, lemon and salt. Cover and cook until it opens.

We serve the turkeys with their sauce.

Lies

Cleaning involves soaking the bivalves in cold, highly salted water to remove any sand and dirt.

ALL OF PEBRE MONKFISH CREATES ME

INGREDIENTS

Because of the fish juice

15 shrimp heads and bodies

1 devil tail head or white fish or 2 bones

Ketchup

1 small onion

1 pair

Salt

for cooking

1 large monkfish tail (or 2 small)

shrimp bodies

1 tablespoon sweet paprika

8 cloves of garlic

4 large potatoes

3 slices of bread

1 cayenne

unpeeled almonds

Olive oil

Salt and pepper

eMPLOYMENT

Because of the fish juice

Cook the fish stock while frying the shrimp bodies and tomato sauce. Add the monkfish bones or head and chopped vegetables. Pour water and boil for 20 min. Drain and season with salt.

for cooking

Fry the uncut garlic in a pan. Remove and reserve. Fry the almonds in the same oil. Remove and reserve.

Fry the bread in the same oil. Withdrawal.

Crush the garlic, a handful of whole unpeeled almonds, the bread slices and the cayenne pepper in a mortar and pestle.

Lightly fry the pepper in the garlic oil, being careful not to burn it, and add it to the broth.

Add the baked potatoes and cook until soft. Add the seasoned monkfish and cook for 3 minutes. Add the chopped prawns and cook for another 2 minutes until the sauce thickens. Season with salt and serve hot.

Lies

Use enough smoke to cover the potatoes. The most common fish used in this recipe is eel, but it can be made with any meaty fish such as turbot or eel.

SHAVED STITCH

INGREDIENTS

1 carp cleaned, deveined and decalcified

25 g of bread crumbs

2 cloves of garlic

1 chili pepper

vinegar

Olive oil

Salt

eMPLOYMENT

Salt and rub oil inside and out. Sprinkle breadcrumbs on top and bake at 180ºC for 25 minutes.

Meanwhile, fry the garlic and the chopped chili on medium heat. Remove a splash of vinegar from the heat and coat the carp with this sauce.

Lies

Forgery is making cuts across the width of the fish to cook it faster.

NAVY CLAMS

INGREDIENTS

1 kg of clams

1 small glass of white wine

1 tablespoon of flour

2 cloves of garlic

1 small tomato

1 onion

½ chili pepper

Food coloring or saffron (optional)

Olive oil

Salt

eMPLOYMENT

Soak the clams for several hours in cold water with plenty of salt to remove any possible soil residue.

After cleaning them, boil the clams in wine and ¼ liter of water. Once they open, remove and reserve the juice.

Cut the onion, garlic and tomatoes into small pieces and fry them in a little oil. Add the chilies and cook until well cooked.

Add a spoonful of flour and cook for another 2 minutes. Rinse with water obtained from boiling the clams. Cook for 10 minutes and add salt. Add the clams and cook for another minute. Now add the dye or saffron.

Lies

Sweet wine can be replaced with white wine. The sauce is very good.

MELUX WITH PEPPER

INGREDIENTS

4 or 5 unsalted cod fillets

4 cloves of garlic

1 chili pepper

½ liter of olive oil

eMPLOYMENT

Fry the garlic and chilli in olive oil over low heat. Remove them and let the oil drain a little.

Place the cod fillet skin side up and cook for 1 minute on low heat. Turn and leave for another 3 minutes. It is important that it is cooked in oil and not fried.

Remove the cod, gradually pour in the oil until only the white substance released by the cod (gelatin) remains.

Take it off the heat and beat it with a colander with a few movements or circular movements while gradually adding the strained oil. Collect the pulp for 10 minutes without stopping mixing.

When ready, add the cod again and stir for another minute.

Lies

To give it a different tone, add a ham bone or some aromatic herbs to the oil in which the cod is fried.

CHICKEN DAPOLE WITH EVERYTHING

INGREDIENTS

12 chicken thighs

200 ml of cream

150 ml of whiskey

100 ml of chicken stock

3 egg yolks

1 small onion

flour

Olive oil

Salt and pepper

eMPLOYMENT

Dust them with flour and fry the chicken thighs. Remove and reserve.

Fry the finely chopped onion in the same oil for 5 minutes. Add whiskey and flambé (cap must be removed). Pour in the cream and stock. Add the chicken again and cook for 20 minutes on low heat.

Remove from the heat, add the yolks and mix carefully so that the sauce thickens a little. Season with salt and pepper if needed.

Lies

Whiskey can be substituted with our favorite alcoholic drink.

ROASTED DUCK

INGREDIENTS

1 clean duck

1 liter of chicken stock

4 dl soy sauce

3 spoons of honey

2 cloves of garlic

1 small onion

1 cayenne

fresh ginger

Olive oil

Salt and pepper

eMPLOYMENT

In a bowl, mix the chicken broth, soy, minced garlic, cayenne pepper and finely chopped onion, honey, a piece of minced ginger and pepper. Marinate the duck in this mixture for 1 hour.

Remove from the marinade and place in a baking dish with half of the marinade liquid. We bake it at 200 degrees for 10 minutes on each side. Constantly wet brush.

Lower the oven to 180ºC and cook for another 18 minutes on each side (brush every 5 minutes).

Remove and reserve the duck and reduce the sauce by half in a saucepan over medium heat.

Lies

First, cook the poultry breast side down so that they are less dry and more juicy.

CHICKEN BODY VILLAROY

INGREDIENTS

1 kg of chicken breast

2 carrots

2 celery sticks

1 onion

1 pair

1 turnip

Flour, eggs and breadcrumbs (for coating)

For the béchamel

1 liter of milk

100 g of butter

100 g of flour

ground nutmeg

Salt and pepper

eMPLOYMENT

Boil all clean vegetables in 2 liters of water (cold) for 45 minutes.

Meanwhile, we make the bechamel by frying the flour in butter on medium-low heat for 5 minutes. Then pour the milk and mix. Drain and add nutmeg. Cook for 10 minutes on low heat, stirring constantly.

Drain the liquid and boil the breasts (whole or fillets) in it for 15 minutes. We take them out and let them cool. Coat the breasts well with the bechamel sauce and put them in the refrigerator. Once cooled, roll in flour, then in egg and finally in breadcrumbs. Fry in plenty of oil and serve hot.

Lies

You can make a unique cream from meat broth and chopped vegetables.

CHICKEN CROWN WITH LEMON MUSTARD SAUCE

INGREDIENTS

4 chicken breasts

250 ml of cream

3 spoons of brandy

3 spoons of mustard

1 tablespoon of flour

2 cloves of garlic

1 lemon

½ onion

Olive oil

Salt and pepper

eMPLOYMENT

Salt the breasts cut into regular pieces and fry in a little oil. Reserve.

Fry the finely chopped onion and garlic in the same oil. Add the flour and cook for 1 min. Pour the brandy until it evaporates, add the cream, 3 tablespoons of lemon juice and its peel, mustard and salt. Cook the sauce for 5 minutes.

Put the chicken back in and cook on low heat for another 5 minutes.

Lies

Before extracting the juice, grate the lemon. To save money, it can also be made with sliced chicken instead of breast.

PINTADA PROVIDED WITH CUMBLES AND MUSHROOMS

INGREDIENTS

1 painted

250 g of mushrooms

Porta 200 ml

¼ liter chicken stock

15 plums with seeds

1 clove of garlic

1 teaspoon of flour

Olive oil

Salt and pepper

eMPLOYMENT

Season with salt and pepper and bake the chickens together with the plums for 40 minutes at 175ºC. Turn halfway through cooking. When the time is up, remove the liquid and reserve.

Fry 2 tablespoons of oil and flour in a pot for 1 minute. Deglaze with wine and let reduce by half. Moisten with steak juices and gravy. Cook for 5 minutes without stopping stirring.

Saute the mushrooms separately with some minced garlic, add to the sauce and let it boil. Serve the poultry with the sauce.

Lies

On special occasions, you can stuff the birds with apples, foie gras, minced meat and dried fruit.

 AVES

VILLAROY chicken breast stuffed with PIQUILLOS caramelized with MODENA vinegar

INGREDIENTS

4 chicken breast fillets

100 g of butter

100 g of flour

1 liter of milk

1 can piquillo peppers

1 glass of Modena vinegar

½ cup of sugar

Nutmeg

Eggs and breadcrumbs (for spread)

Olive oil

Salt and pepper

eMPLOYMENT

Fry the butter and flour over low heat for 10 minutes. Then pour the milk and cook for 20 minutes, stirring constantly. Drain and add nutmeg. Let it cool.

Meanwhile, caramelize the peppers with the vinegar and sugar until the vinegar starts (just starts) to thicken.

Arrange the fillet and fill it with piquillo. Wrap the breasts in cling film as if they were very hard candies, seal and boil in water for 15 minutes.

When it is baked, brush it with bechamel on all sides and coat it with beaten egg and breadcrumbs. Fry in plenty of oil.

Lies

If we add a couple of spoons of curry to the flour for bechamel, we get a different and very rich result.

CHICKEN STUFFED WITH HAM, MUSHROOMS AND CHEESE

INGREDIENTS

4 chicken breast fillets

100 g of mushrooms

4 slices of smoked ham

2 spoons of mustard

6 spoons of cream

1 onion

1 clove of garlic

sliced cheese

Olive oil

Salt and pepper

eMPLOYMENT

Season chicken fillet. Clean the mushrooms and cut them into quarters.

Fry the bacon and fry the minced mushrooms with garlic over high heat.

Fill the fillets with bacon, cheese and mushrooms and seal them perfectly with cling film, as if they were candy. Cook for 10 minutes in boiling water. Remove the film and fillet.

On the other hand, fry the onion cut into small pieces, add the cream and mustard, cook for 2 minutes and mix. Sauce on chicken

Lies

The transparent film maintains a high temperature and does not impart any taste to the food.

CHICKEN IN SWEET PLUM WINE

INGREDIENTS

1 large chicken

100 g of plums without seeds

½ liter of chicken broth

½ bottle of sweet wine

1 small onion

2 carrots

1 clove of garlic

1 tablespoon of flour

Olive oil

Salt and pepper

eMPLOYMENT

Arrange and fry the chicken pieces in a very hot pot with oil. Take out and reserve.

Fry the onion, garlic and finely chopped carrots in the same oil. When the vegetables are cooked well, add the flour and cook for another minute.

Deglaze with sweet wine and increase heat until almost completely reduced. Brush with liquid and add the chicken and prunes.

Bake for about 15 minutes or until the chicken is tender. Remove the chicken and stir in the sauce. Adjust it with salt.

Lies

If you add a little cold butter to the minced sauce and beat it with a whisk, it will thicken and become glossy.

Orange chicken breast with cashew nuts

INGREDIENTS

4 chicken breasts

75 g of cashews

2 cups of fresh orange juice

4 spoons of honey

2 tablespoons Cointreau

flour

Olive oil

Salt and pepper

eMPLOYMENT

Season the breast with spices and flour. Fry them in plenty of oil, take them out and leave them.

Boil orange juice with Cointreau and honey for 5 minutes. Add the brisket to the sauce and cook over low heat for 8 minutes.

Serve with sauce and cashews on top.

Lies

Another way to make a good orange sauce is to start with a not too dark caramel and add natural orange juice.

marinated partridge

INGREDIENTS

4 quails

300 g of onion

200 g of carrots

2 glasses of white wine

1 head of garlic

1 bay leaf

1 glass of vinegar

1 glass of oil

salt and 10 pepper

eMPLOYMENT

Arrange and fry the quails over high heat. Remove and reserve.

Fry the carrots and onions in the same oil. When the vegetables have softened, add the wine, vinegar, peppercorns, salt, garlic and bay leaf. Boil for 10 min.

Put the quail back and cook on low heat for another 10 minutes.

Lies

In order for marinated meat or fish to take on more flavor, it is best to let them rest for at least 24 hours.

COCKTAIL CHICKEN

INGREDIENTS

1 minced chicken

50 g sliced mushrooms

½ liter of chicken broth

1 glass of white wine

4 chopped tomatoes

2 carrots

2 cloves of garlic

1 pair

½ onion

1 bunch of aromatic herbs (thyme, rosemary, bay leaves...)

Olive oil

Salt and pepper

eMPLOYMENT

Arrange and fry the chicken in a very hot pot with a little oil. Take out and reserve.

Fry the diced carrots, garlic, leek and onion in the same oil. Then add the chopped tomato. Boil until the tomato loses its water. Put the chicken back in.

Saute the mushrooms separately and add them to the stew. Take a bath with a glass of wine and let it cool down.

Brush with broth and add aromatic herbs. Cook until the chicken is tender. Adjust the salt.

Lies

This dish can be made with turkey and even rabbit.

COCA COLA style chicken wings

INGREDIENTS

1 kg of chicken wings

½ liter Coca-Cola

4 spoons of brown sugar

2 spoons of soy sauce

1 level spoon of oregano

½ lemon

Salt and pepper

eMPLOYMENT

Add Coca-Cola, sugar, soy, oregano and juice of ½ lemon to a saucepan and boil for 2 minutes.

Cut the wings in half and sprinkle with salt. Bake at 160 ºC until they take color. Meanwhile, pour half of the sauce and turn the wings. Turn them every 20 minutes.

When the sauce has almost reduced, add the other side and continue cooking until the sauce thickens.

Lies

When making a sauce, adding a sprig of vanilla enhances the flavor and gives it a unique feel.

GARLIC CHICKEN

INGREDIENTS

1 minced chicken

8 cloves of garlic

1 glass of white wine

1 tablespoon of flour

1 cayenne

vinegar

Olive oil

Salt and pepper

eMPLOYMENT

We fix the chicken and fry it well. Reserve and let the oil cool.

Chop the garlic cloves and mince (fry in oil, don't fry) the garlic and cayenne so they don't color.

Rinse with wine and allow to reduce to a certain thickness but not dry.

Then add the chicken meat and add a few spoons of flour on top. Stir (check if the garlic sticks to the chicken; if not, add a little more flour until it sticks a bit).

Cover and stir occasionally. Cook for 20 minutes on low heat. Finish with a splash of vinegar and cook for another 1 minute.

Lies

Boiling the chicken is a must. It should be on very high heat to keep it golden on the outside and juicy on the inside.

CHICKEN CHILINDRÓN

INGREDIENTS

1 small chicken, diced

350 g chopped Serrano ham

1 can with 800 g of chopped tomatoes

1 large red pepper

1 large green pepper

1 large onion

2 cloves of garlic

Thyme

1 glass of white or red wine

sugar

Olive oil

Salt and pepper

eMPLOYMENT

Arrange the chicken and cook it on high heat. Take out and reserve.

In the same oil, fry the pepper, garlic and onion cut into medium pieces. When the vegetables are fried well, add the ham and cook for another 10 minutes.

Put the chicken back in and brush with wine. Leave for 5 minutes on high heat and add the tomato and thyme. Lower the heat and cook for another 30 minutes. Adjust salt and sugar.

Lies

The same recipe can be made with meatballs. Nothing will be left on the plate!

pickled beans AND RED FRUITS

INGREDIENTS

4 quails

150 g of red fruit

1 glass of vinegar

2 glasses of white wine

1 carrot

1 pair

1 clove of garlic

1 bay leaf

flour

1 glass of oil

Salt and pepper

eMPLOYMENT

We spray, arrange and fry the quail in a pot. Take out and reserve.

In the same oil, fry the carrot and leek cut into cubes and the garlic cut into slices. When the vegetables have softened, add the oil, vinegar and wine.

Add bay leaves and pepper. Adjust them with salt and boil them for 10 minutes together with the red fruits.

Add the quails and cook for another 10 minutes until tender. Keep covered from heat.

Lies

This marinade, along with quail meat, is an excellent sauce and addition to a good hearty salad.

LEMON CHICKEN

INGREDIENTS

1 chicken

30 g of sugar

25 g of butter

1 liter of chicken stock

1 dl white wine

Juice of 3 lemons

1 onion

1 pair

Olive oil

Salt and pepper

eMPLOYMENT

Cut the chicken and season. Toast over high heat and remove.

Peel the onion, clean the leek and cut into strips. Fry the vegetables in the same oil as the chicken. Wash with wine and let it reduce.

Add lemon juice, sugar and juice. Cook for 5 minutes and add the chicken back. Cook on low heat for another 30 minutes. Season with salt and pepper.

Lies

To make the sauce finer and without pieces of vegetables, it is better to chop it.

CHICKEN SAN JACOBO WITH SERRANO COMPOUND, CASAR CAKE AND ROCKET

INGREDIENTS

8 thin chicken fillets

150 g of Casar cake

100 g of arugula

4 slices serrano ham

Flour, eggs and cereals (for coating)

Olive oil

Salt and pepper

eMPLOYMENT

Arrange the chicken fillet and cover it with cheese. Place arugula and Serrano ham on top of one and top with another to close. Do the same with the rest.

Pour in the flour, beaten eggs and crushed flakes. Fry in plenty of hot oil for 3 minutes.

Lies

It can be topped with crushed popcorn, kikos and even earthworms. The result is very funny.

BREADED CHICKEN BACK

INGREDIENTS

4 chicken thighs (per person)

1 liter of cream

1 onion or scallion

2 tablespoons of curry

4 natural yogurts

Salt

eMPLOYMENT

Cut the onion into small pieces and mix it with yogurt, cream and curry in a bowl. Season with salt.

Cut the chicken and marinate it in sour cream for 24 hours.

Bake at 180ºC for 90 minutes, remove the chicken and serve with whipped sauce.

Lies

If the sauce is left, you can make delicious meatballs from it.

CHICKEN IN RED WINE

INGREDIENTS

1 minced chicken

½ liter of red wine

1 sprig of rosemary

1 sprig of thyme

2 cloves of garlic

2 pairs

1 red pepper

1 carrot

1 onion

Chicken soup

flour

Olive oil

Salt and pepper

eMPLOYMENT

Arrange and cook the chicken in a very hot pan. Take out and reserve.

Cut the vegetables into small pieces and fry them in the same oil as the chicken.

Wash with wine, add aromatic herbs and cook for about 10 minutes on high heat until softened. Add the chicken back in and baste with the stock until covered. Bake for another 20 minutes or until the meat is tender.

Lies

For a thinner sauce without lumps, grate and strain the sauce.

BLACK BEER GRILLED CHICKEN

INGREDIENTS

4 chicken thighs

750 ml dark beer

1 spoon cumin

1 sprig of thyme

1 sprig of rosemary

2 onions

3 cloves of garlic

1 carrot

Salt and pepper

eMPLOYMENT

Cut the onions, carrots and garlic into julienne. Place the thyme and rosemary in the bottom of the pan and top with the onion, carrots and garlic; and then chicken thighs, skin side down, seasoned with a pinch of cumin. Bake at 175 ºC for about 45 minutes.

After 30 minutes, moisten with beer, turn the bottom and bake for another 45 minutes. When the chicken is cooked, remove from the pan and stir in the sauce.

Lies

If you put 2 sliced apples in the middle of the steak and mash them with the rest of the sauce, it tastes even better.

CHOCOLATE partridge

INGREDIENTS

4 quails

½ liter of chicken broth

½ glass of red wine

1 sprig of rosemary

1 sprig of thyme

1 small onion

1 carrot

1 clove of garlic

1 chopped tomato

Chocolate

Olive oil

Salt and pepper

eMPLOYMENT

We arrange and fry the quails. Reserve.

In the same oil, fry the finely chopped carrots, garlic and onion over medium heat. Increase the heat and add the tomato. Boil until the water evaporates. Wash with wine and let it reduce almost completely.

Brush with gravy and add herbs. Cook over low heat until the quails are tender. Adjust the salt. Remove from heat and add chocolate to taste. Remove.

Lies

You can add cayenne pepper to add some spice to the dish, or add hazelnuts or toasted almonds to prepare.

Calcutta Lark SERVED WITH RED FRUIT SAUCE

INGREDIENTS

4 turkey legs

250 g of red fruit

½ liter of cava

1 sprig of thyme

1 sprig of rosemary

3 cloves of garlic

2 pairs

1 carrot

Olive oil

Salt and pepper

eMPLOYMENT

Wash and clean the leeks, carrots and garlic. Place this vegetable in a baking dish along with the thyme, rosemary and red berries.

Place the turkey quarters on top, season with a little oil, skin side down. Bake at 175ºC for 1 hour.

Take a cava shower after 30 minutes. Turn the meat over and cook for another 45 minutes. When the time is up, remove it from the box. Mix, strain and put the sauce with salt.

Lies

The turkey is done when the thighs and thighs separate easily.

SAFE CHICKEN WITH PEACH SAUCE

INGREDIENTS

4 chicken thighs

½ liter of white wine

1 sprig of thyme

1 sprig of rosemary

3 cloves of garlic

2 peaches

2 onions

1 carrot

Olive oil

Salt and pepper

eMPLOYMENT

Cut the onions, carrots and garlic into julienne. Peel the peaches, cut them in half and remove the pit.

Add the thyme and rosemary to the bottom of the pan along with the carrots, onions and garlic. Place the backs on top, arrange them with a little oil, skin side down, and bake them at 175°C for about 45 minutes.

After 30 minutes, rinse with white wine, turn and cook for another 45 minutes. When the chicken is cooked, remove from the pan and stir in the sauce.

Lies

You can add apples or pears to the steak. The sauce will taste great.

CHICKEN FILLET STUFFED WITH SPINACH AND MOZARELA

INGREDIENTS

8 thin chicken fillets

200 g of fresh spinach

150 grams of mozzarella

8 basil leaves

1 teaspoon ground cumin

Flour, eggs and breadcrumbs (for coating)

Olive oil

Salt and pepper

eMPLOYMENT

Season the breast on both sides. Place spinach, grated cheese and chopped basil on top, cover with another fillet. Top with the flour, beaten egg and breadcrumbs and cumin mixture.

Cook for a few minutes on each side and remove excess oil on absorbent paper.

Lies

A good addition is a good tomato sauce. This dish can be made with turkey and even fresh fillets.

INSURED CHICKEN WITH CAVA

INGREDIENTS

4 chicken thighs

1 bottle of cava

1 sprig of thyme

1 sprig of rosemary

3 cloves of garlic

2 onions

Olive oil

Salt and pepper

eMPLOYMENT

Cut the onions and julienne garlic. Place the thyme and rosemary in the bottom of the pan, skin side down, and add the onions, garlic and seasoned hind legs. Bake at 175 ºC for about 45 minutes.

After 30 minutes, wash with kava, turn and bake for another 45 minutes. When the chicken is cooked, remove from the pan and stir in the sauce.

Lies

Another variation of the same recipe is to make it with lambrusco or sweet wine.

CHICKEN WITH WALNUT SALUS

INGREDIENTS

600 g of chicken breast

150 g of peanuts

500 ml of chicken stock

200 ml of cream

3 spoons of soy sauce

3 spoons of honey

1 tablespoon curry

1 finely ground cayenne

1 tablespoon of lemon juice

Olive oil

Salt and pepper

eMPLOYMENT

Grind the peanuts very well until they become a paste. Mix together in a bowl with lemon juice, stock, soy, honey, curry, salt and pepper. Cut the breast into pieces and marinate in this mixture overnight.

Remove the chicken and place on a skewer. Cook the previous mixture together with the cream on low heat for 10 minutes.

Fry the skewers in a pan over medium heat and serve with the sauce on top.

Lies

They can be made with chicken thighs. But instead of baking it in a pan, bake it in the oven with the sauce on top.

CHICKEN PEPTITOR

INGREDIENTS

1 ½ kg of chicken

250 g of onion

50 g of roasted almonds

25 g of baked bread

½ liter of chicken broth

¼ liter of good wine

2 cloves of garlic

2 bay leaves

2 hard boiled eggs

1 tablespoon of flour

14 strands of saffron

150 g of olive oil

Salt and pepper

eMPLOYMENT

Cut and arrange the chicken cut into pieces. Brown and reserved.

Cut the onion and garlic into small pieces and fry them in the same oil with which the chicken was fried. Add the flour and cook over low heat for 5 minutes. Wash with wine and let it reduce.

Brush with salted gravy and cook for another 15 minutes. Then add the chicken along with the bay leaves and cook until the chicken is tender.

Fry the saffron separately and add it to the mortar together with toasted bread, almonds and egg yolks. Mix until you have a paste and add to the chicken stew. Cook another 5 minutes.

Lies

There is no better addition to this recipe than a good rice pilaf. It can be served with beaten egg whites and topped with some finely chopped parsley.

ORANGE CHICKEN

INGREDIENTS

1 chicken

25 g of butter

1 liter of chicken stock

1 dl rose wine

2 spoons of honey

1 sprig of thyme

2 carrots

2 oranges

2 pairs

Olive oil

Salt and pepper

eMPLOYMENT

Drop and fry the minced chicken in olive oil over high heat. Remove and reserve.

Peel the carrots and leeks, clean them and cut them into julienne strips. Fry in the same oil as the chicken. Cover with wine and cook over high heat until tender.

Add the orange juice, honey and juice. Cook for 5 minutes and add the chicken pieces again. Simmer on low heat for 30 minutes. Add cold butter and season with salt and pepper.

Lies

You can skip a good handful of nuts and add them to the stew at the end of cooking.

Chicken Stew WITH BERAGE

INGREDIENTS

1 chicken

200 g serran ham

200 grams of boletus

50 g of butter

600 ml of chicken stock

1 glass of white wine

1 sprig of thyme

1 clove of garlic

1 carrot

1 onion

1 tomato

Olive oil

Salt and pepper

eMPLOYMENT

Cut the chicken, season and fry in butter and a little oil. Remove and reserve.

In the same fat, fry the onion, carrot and garlic cut into small pieces together with the diced ham. Turn up the heat and add the minced bull. Cook for 2 minutes, add the chopped tomatoes and cook until the water evaporates.

Add the chicken pieces back in and rinse with wine. Reduce until the sauce is almost dry. Moisten with gravy and add thyme. Simmer for 25 minutes or until the chicken is tender. Adjust the salt.

Lies

Use seasonal or dehydrated mushrooms.

ROASTED CHICKEN WITH NUTS AND SOY

INGREDIENTS

3 chicken breasts

70 g of raisins

30 grams of almonds

30 g of cashews

30 g of walnuts

30 grams of hazelnuts

1 cup chicken broth

3 spoons of soy sauce

2 cloves of garlic

1 cayenne

1 lemon

Ginger

Olive oil

Salt and pepper

eMPLOYMENT

Cut the breast, salt, pepper and fry in a pan over high heat. Remove and reserve.

In that oil, fry the walnuts together with minced garlic, a piece of minced ginger, cayenne pepper and lemon zest.

Add raisins, chicken breast and soy. Lower to 1 min. and rinse with broth. Cook for another 6 minutes on medium heat and add salt if necessary.

Lies

You will practically not need to use salt because it consists almost entirely of soybeans.

CHOCOLATE CHICKEN WITH ROASTED ALMONDS

INGREDIENTS

1 chicken

60 g of chopped dark chocolate

1 glass of red wine

1 sprig of thyme

1 sprig of rosemary

1 bay leaf

2 carrots

2 cloves of garlic

1 onion

Chicken stock (or water)

Roasted almonds

extra virgin olive oil

Salt and pepper

eMPLOYMENT

Cut the chicken, season and cook in a very hot pot. Remove and reserve.

In the same oil, fry the onion, carrots and garlic cloves cut into small pieces over low heat.

Add bay leaves and sprigs of thyme and rosemary. Pour in the wine and stock and simmer over low heat for 40 minutes. Sprinkle with salt and remove the chicken.

Pour the sauce into a blender and return to the pot. Add the chicken and chocolate and stir until the chocolate melts. Cook for another 5 minutes to blend the flavors.

Lies

Top with toasted almonds. Adding cayenne or chili peppers gives it a spiciness.

LAMB KABS WITH PEPPERS AND PINEAPPLE VINEGAR

INGREDIENTS

350 g of lamb

2 tablespoons of vinegar

1 spoon paprika

1 level spoon of mustard

1 spoon of sugar

1 tray of cherry tomatoes

1 green pepper

1 red pepper

1 small onion

1 onion

5 tablespoons of olive oil

Salt and pepper

eMPLOYMENT

Clean the vegetables, except the onions, and cut them into medium squares. Cut the lamb into cubes of the same size. Assemble the skewers by alternating a piece of meat and a piece of vegetables. The season. Fry them in a very hot pan with a little oil for 1 or 2 minutes on each side.

Mix the mustard, paprika, sugar, oil, vinegar and chopped onion in a separate bowl. Season with salt and emulsify.

Serve the freshly made skewers with a little paprika sauce.

Lies

You can also add 1 tablespoon of curry and some lemon peel to the vinaigrette.

VICHI SMOKE FILLED IN PORT

INGREDIENTS

1 kg of veal feathers (open the booklet to fill)

350 g of minced pork

1 kg of carrots

1 kg of onion

100 g of pine nuts

1 small can piquillo peppers

1 can of black olives

1 package of bacon

1 head of garlic

2 bay leaves

port wine

Broth

Olive oil

Salt and pepper

eMPLOYMENT

The season ends on both sides. Top with pork, pine nuts, sliced bell peppers, quartered olives, and bacon strips. Roll up and place in a net or tie with bridle string. Toasted on very high heat, remove and set aside.

Cut the carrots, onions and garlic into slices and fry them in the same oil in which the beef was fried. Put fin again. Drizzle with a splash of port and gravy until all is covered. Add 8 peppercorns and bay leaves. Cook covered on low heat for 40 minutes. Turn every 10 minutes. When the meat is tender, take it out and mix the sauce.

Lies

Any other wine or champagne can be substituted for the port wine.

MADRLEJA

INGREDIENTS

1 kg of ground beef

500 g ground pork

500 g of ripe tomatoes

150 g of onion

100 g of mushrooms

1 l broth (or water)

2 dl white wine

2 tablespoons of fresh parsley

2 tablespoons of breadcrumbs

1 tablespoon of flour

3 cloves of garlic

2 carrots

1 bay leaf

1 egg

sugar

Olive oil

Salt and pepper

eMPLOYMENT

Mix both meats with chopped parsley, 2 cloves of garlic cut into cubes, breadcrumbs, egg, salt and pepper. Form balls and fry them in a pan. Take out and reserve.

Fry the onion with another garlic in the same oil, add flour and fry. Add the tomatoes and fry for another 5 minutes. Wash with wine and cook another 10 minutes. Cover with meat broth and continue cooking for another 5 minutes. Grind and adjust the salt and sugar. Boil the meatballs in the sauce for 10 minutes together with the bay leaf.

Clean, peel and cut carrots and mushrooms separately. Fry them in a little oil for 2 minutes and add them to the meatball stew.

Lies

For a tastier meatball mix, add 150g of fresh chopped Iberian ham. When making the balls, it is best not to press too much to make them more liquid.

CHOCOLATE WALNUT DOUBLE

INGREDIENTS

8 sides of beef

½ liter of red wine

6 ounces of chocolate

2 cloves of garlic

2 tomatoes

2 pairs

1 celery stick

1 carrot

1 onion

1 sprig of rosemary

1 sprig of thyme

flour

Beef jerky (or water)

Olive oil

Salt and pepper

eMPLOYMENT

Drop and brown the cheeks in a very hot pot. Take out and reserve.

Cut the vegetables into small pieces and sauté them in the same pot in which the cheeks were fried.

When the vegetables are soft, add the chopped tomatoes and cook until all the water is gone. Add the wine, aromatic herbs and leave for 5 minutes. Toss the cheeks and gravy until covered.

Cook until the cheeks are very soft, add chocolate to taste, mix and season with salt and pepper.

Lies

The sauce can be pureed or left with whole pieces of vegetables.

CONFIT MEAT CAKE WITH SWEET WINE SAUCE

INGREDIENTS

½ minced pork

1 glass of sweet wine

2 sprigs of rosemary

2 sprigs of thyme

4 cloves of garlic

1 small carrot

1 small onion

1 tomato

mild olive oil

coarse salt

eMPLOYMENT

Lay the breast pork on a tray and salt both sides. Add minced garlic and aromatics. Brush it with oil and bake it at 100ºC for 5 hours. Then let it cool and remove the bones, removing the flesh and skin.

Place parchment paper on a baking sheet. Separate the pork belly and place the skin of the pork belly on top (it should be at least 2 fingers high). Place another sheet of parchment paper and refrigerate with a weight on top.

Meanwhile, bring the dark stock to a boil. Cut the bones and vegetables into medium pieces. Bake the bones at 185ºC for 35 minutes, put the vegetables on the side and bake for another 25 minutes. Remove from the oven and cover with wine. Put everything in a pot and cover with cold water. Cook for 2 hours on very low heat. Drain and return to heat until slightly thickened. Degrease.

Cut the pie into pieces and fry in a hot pan on the skin side until brown. Bake for 3 minutes at 180ºC.

Lies

It's more of a chore than a complicated dish, but the result is impressive. The only trick to not ruining the bottom is to serve the sauce on one side of the meat, not on top.

RABBIT WITH PUPPIES

INGREDIENTS

1 sliced rabbit

80 grams of almonds

1 liter of chicken stock

400 ml pomace

200 ml of cream

1 sprig of rosemary

1 sprig of thyme

2 onions

2 cloves of garlic

1 carrot

10 strands of saffron

Salt and pepper

eMPLOYMENT

Cut, trim and fry the rabbit. Remove and reserve.

Fry the carrot, onion and garlic cut into small pieces in the same oil. Add saffron and almonds and cook for 1 min.

Turn up the heat and make a pomace bath. flambé Add the rabbit back in and baste with the liquid. Add the sprigs of thyme and rosemary.

Cook for about 30 minutes until the rabbit is tender and pour the cream. Cook for another 5 minutes and remove the salt.

Lies

Flambear burns souls. Be sure to turn off the hood when doing this.

MEAT BALLS IN PEPITORIA HAZELNUT SAUCE

INGREDIENTS

750 g ground beef

750 g of ground pork

250 g of onion

60 g of hazelnuts

25 g of baked bread

½ liter of chicken broth

¼ liter of white wine

10 strands of saffron

2 tablespoons of fresh parsley

2 tablespoons of breadcrumbs

4 cloves of garlic

2 hard boiled eggs

1 fresh egg

2 bay leaves

150 g of olive oil

Salt and pepper

eMPLOYMENT

In a bowl, mix the meat, chopped parsley, diced garlic, breadcrumbs, egg, salt and pepper. Toast the flour in a saucepan over medium-high heat. Remove and reserve.

In the same oil, gently fry the onion and the other 2 cloves of garlic cut into small cubes. Wash with wine and let it reduce. Brush with gravy and cook for 15 minutes. Add the meatballs to the sauce along with the bay leaves and cook for another 15 minutes.

Fry the saffron separately and grind in a mortar together with the fried bread, hazelnuts and egg yolks until you get a soft paste. Add to the stew and cook for another 5 minutes.

Lies

Serve with beaten egg whites on top and some parsley.

MEAT STICKS WITH DARK BEER

INGREDIENTS

4 beef fillets

125 g of shiitake mushrooms

1/3 liter dark beer

1 dl meat broth

1 dl of cream

1 carrot

1 small onion

1 tomato

1 sprig of thyme

1 sprig of rosemary

flour

Olive oil

Salt and pepper

eMPLOYMENT

Arrange the fillet and sprinkle it with flour. Lightly fry them in a pan with a little oil. Take out and reserve.

Fry the diced onion and carrot in the same oil. When they are cooked, add the chopped tomatoes and cook until the sauce is almost dry.

Wash with beer, let the alcohol evaporate for 5 minutes on medium heat and add the broth, herbs and fillet. Cook for 15 minutes or until tender.

Fry the fillet mushrooms separately on high heat and add them to the stew. Adjust the salt.

Lies

The fillet should not be overcooked, otherwise it will be too tough.

TRIP TO MADRLEÑA

INGREDIENTS

1 kg of clean rice

2 pork wheels

25 g of flour

1 dl of vinegar

2 spoons of paprika

2 bay leaves

2 onions (1 of them spiked)

1 head of garlic

1 chili pepper

2 dl olive oil

20 g of salt

eMPLOYMENT

Blanch the whip and pork in a pot of cold water. Once it starts boiling, cook for 5 minutes.

Drain and fill with clean water. Add the onion, chilli, garlic head and bay leaves. Add more water if necessary to cover well and simmer covered for 4 hours or until the trotters are tender.

When the triplets are ready, remove the onion, bay leaf and chili pepper. Remove the trotters as well, debone them and cut them into bite-sized pieces. Put it back in the pot.

Separately fry another onion cut in brunoise, add paprika and 1 spoon of flour. Once it's cooked, put it on the boil. Cook for 5 minutes, season with salt and add thickener if needed.

Lies

This recipe takes on flavor if made a day or two ahead. You can also add some boiled chickpeas and get a first class vegetable dish.

PORK'S FEET WITH APPLE AND MINT

INGREDIENTS

800 g of fresh pork

500 g of apples

60 g of sugar

1 glass of white wine

1 glass of brandy

10 mint leaves

1 bay leaf

1 large onion

1 carrot

Olive oil

Salt and pepper

eMPLOYMENT

Spray the fillet and cook over high heat. Remove and reserve.

Fry the cleaned and finely chopped onion and carrot in that oil. Peel the apples and remove the core.

Transfer everything to a baking tray, sprinkle with alcohol and add a bay leaf. Bake at 185ºC for 90 min.

Remove the apples and vegetables, grate them with sugar and mint. Pour the cooking juices over the fillet and sauce and serve with the apple compote.

Lies

To prevent the fillet from drying out, add a little water to the pan while cooking.

CHICKEN BALLS WITH RASPBERRY SAUCE

INGREDIENTS

for meatballs

1 kg of ground chicken

1 dl of milk

2 tablespoons of breadcrumbs

2 eggs

1 clove of garlic

sherry wine

flour

Chopped parsley

Olive oil

Salt and pepper

For the raspberry sauce

200 g of raspberry jam

½ l chicken broth

1 ½ dl white wine

½ dl soy sauce

1 tomato

2 carrots

1 clove of garlic

1 onion

Salt

eMPLOYMENT

for meatballs

Mix the meat with the breadcrumbs, milk, eggs, a finely minced garlic clove, parsley and a splash of wine. Season with salt and pepper and let it stand for 15 minutes.

Shape the mixture into balls and pass them through the flour. Fry in oil so that it is slightly green inside. Reserve the oil.

For the sweet and sour raspberry sauce

Peel the onion, garlic and carrot and cut them into small cubes. Fry in the same oil in which the meatballs were fried. Season with a pinch of salt. Add the chopped tomatoes without skin or seeds and cook until the water evaporates.

Deglaze with wine and cook until reduced by half. Add the soy sauce and stock and cook for another 20 minutes until the sauce thickens. Add the jam and meatballs and cook all together for another 10 minutes.

Lies

Raspberry jam can be replaced with any other red fruit and even jam.

stew with lamb

INGREDIENTS

1 leg of lamb

1 large glass of red wine

½ cup crushed tomatoes (or 2 chopped tomatoes)

1 tablespoon sweet paprika

2 large potatoes

1 green pepper

1 red pepper

1 onion

Beef jerky (or water)

Olive oil

Salt and pepper

eMPLOYMENT

Cut, trim and roast the leg in a very hot pot. Take out and reserve.

In the same oil, fry the pepper and diced onion. When the vegetables are fried well, add a spoonful of paprika and tomatoes. Cook on high heat until the tomato loses its water. Then add the lamb back in.

Wash with wine and let it reduce. Cover with gravy.

Add the potato cacheladas (uncut) when the lamb is tender and cook until the potatoes are done. Season with salt and pepper.

Lies

For an even tastier sauce, fry 4 piquillo peppers and 1 clove of garlic separately. Mix with a little liquid from the stew and pour into the stew.

LAPUR CIVET

INGREDIENTS

1 rabbit

250 g of mushrooms

250 g of carrots

250 g of onion

100 g of ham

¼ liter of red wine

3 spoons of tomato sauce

2 cloves of garlic

2 sprigs of thyme

2 bay leaves

Beef jerky (or water)

Olive oil

Salt and pepper

eMPLOYMENT

Cut the rabbit and marinate for 24 hours in finely chopped carrots, garlic and onions, wine, 1 sprig of thyme and 1 bay leaf. When the time is up, strain and keep the wine on one side and the vegetables on the other.

We arrange the rabbit, fry it on high heat and take it out. Fry the vegetables on medium-low heat in the same oil. Pour the tomato sauce and cook for 3 minutes. Put the rabbit back. Stir in the wine and stock until the meat is coated. Add a sprig of thyme and a bay leaf. Cook until the rabbit is tender.

Meanwhile, sauté the ham cut into strips and the mushrooms cut into quarters and add to the stew. Grind the rabbit liver separately in a mortar and mix as well. Cook for another 10 minutes, add salt and pepper.

Lies

This dish can be prepared with any game and will taste better if you cook it the day before.

RABBIT WITH PEPPER RADA

INGREDIENTS

1 rabbit

2 large tomatoes

2 onions

1 green pepper

1 clove of garlic

sugar

Olive oil

Salt and pepper

eMPLOYMENT

Cut the rabbit, season it and fry it in a hot pot. Remove and reserve.

Cut the onions, peppers and garlic into small pieces and fry them over low heat for 15 minutes in the same oil in which the rabbit was fried.

Add the chopped tomatoes to the pan and cook over medium heat until the water evaporates. Adjust salt and sugar as needed.

Add the rabbit, reduce the heat and cook for 15 to 20 minutes with the pot covered, stirring occasionally.

Lies

Zucchini or eggplant can be added to pepperrad.

CHEESE STUFFED CHICKEN POPULA WITH CURRY SAUCE

INGREDIENTS

500 g of ground chicken

150 g of cheese cut into cubes

100 g of bread crumbs

200 ml of cream

1 cup chicken broth

2 tablespoons of curry

½ tablespoon of breadcrumbs

30 raisins

1 green pepper

1 carrot

1 onion

1 egg

1 lemon

milky

flour

Olive oil

Salt

eMPLOYMENT

Arrange the chicken and mix it with the breadcrumbs, the egg, 1 tablespoon of curry and the breadcrumbs soaked in milk. Form balls, add a cube of cheese and pour the flour. Bake and reserve.

Fry the onion, pepper and carrot cut into small pieces in the same oil. Add the lemon zest and cook for a few minutes. Add another spoonful of curry, raisins and chicken stock. When it starts to boil, pour the cream and cook for 20 minutes. Adjust the salt.

Lies

The ideal accompaniment to these meatballs are quartered mushrooms, fried with a few cloves of garlic, cut into small pieces and washed down with a large Port or Pedro Ximénez wine.

Page PIG IN RED WINE

INGREDIENTS

12 pig pages

½ liter of red wine

2 cloves of garlic

2 pairs

1 red pepper

1 carrot

1 onion

flour

Beef jerky (or water)

Olive oil

Salt and pepper

eMPLOYMENT

Drop and brown the cheeks in a very hot pot. Take out and reserve.

Cut the vegetables into strips and fry them in the same oil as the pork. When they are well boiled, we moisten them with wine and let them contract for 5 minutes. Toss the cheeks and gravy until covered.

Cook until the cheeks are very tender, stirring the sauce if desired to remove any bits of vegetable.

Lies

Pork cheeks take much less time to cook than beef cheeks. Another flavor is achieved by adding an ounce of chocolate to the sauce at the end.

COCHIFRITO NAVARRE

INGREDIENTS

2 sliced lamb legs

50 g of fat

1 teaspoon paprika

1 tablespoon of vinegar

2 cloves of garlic

1 onion

Olive oil

Salt and pepper

eMPLOYMENT

Cut the lamb legs into pieces. Drain and cook in a pot over high heat. Take out and reserve.

Fry the finely chopped onion and garlic in the same oil over low heat for 8 minutes. Add the paprika and fry for another 5 seconds. Add the lamb and cover with water.

Cook until the sauce has reduced and the meat is tender. Moisten with vinegar and bring to a boil.

Lies

Pre-baking is essential as it prevents juices from escaping. In addition, it adds crunch and improves taste.

Beef Stew WITH PEANUT SAUCE

INGREDIENTS

750 g of beef

250 g of peanuts

2 liters of broth

1 glass of cream

½ glass of brandy

2 spoons of tomato sauce

1 sprig of thyme

1 sprig of rosemary

4 potatoes

2 carrots

1 onion

1 clove of garlic

Olive oil

Salt and pepper

eMPLOYMENT

Cut the sticks, season them and roast them over high heat. Take out and reserve.

In the same oil, fry the onion, garlic and carrots cut into small cubes on low heat. Increase the heat and pour in the tomato sauce. Let it reduce until all the water is gone. Sprinkle it with brandy and let the alcohol evaporate. Add the meat back.

Grind the peanuts well with the liquid and add them to the pan together with the aromatic herbs. Cook over low heat until the meat is almost tender.

Then add the peeled and diced potatoes and the cream. Cook for 10 minutes, add salt and pepper. Let rest for 15 minutes before serving.

Lies

Rice pilaf can be served with this meat dish (see Rice and pasta section).

ROASTED PORK

INGREDIENTS

1 pig is sucking

2 tablespoons lard

Salt

eMPLOYMENT

Line the ears and tail with aluminum foil to prevent burning.

Place 2 wooden spoons in the pan and place the suckling pig face up so that it does not touch the base of the pan. Add 2 spoons of water and bake at 180ºC for 2 hours.

Dissolve the salt in 4 dl of water and coat the inside of the old pig every 10 minutes. At this point, turn it upside down and continue basting with water and salt until the time is up.

Melt the butter and color the skin. Preheat the oven to 200 degrees and bake for another 30 minutes or until the skin is golden and crispy.

Lies

Do not pour the liquid on the skin; so that it loses its sharpness. We serve the sauce on the base of the plate.

CABBAGE INSURED

INGREDIENTS

4 fingers

½ cabbage

3 cloves of garlic

Olive oil

Salt and pepper

eMPLOYMENT

Cover the pots with boiling water and simmer for 2 hours or until completely tender.

Remove them from the water and fry them with a little oil at 220 degrees until golden brown. The season.

Cut the cabbage into thin strips. Cook in boiling water for 15 minutes. Drain it.

Meanwhile, fry the minced garlic in a little oil, add the cabbage and fry. Season with salt and pepper and serve with roasted drumsticks.

Lies

Dumplings can also be made in a very hot pan. Fry them well on all sides.

RABBIT COCKTAIL

INGREDIENTS

1 rabbit

300 g of mushrooms

2 cups of chicken stock

1 glass of white wine

1 sprig of fresh thyme

1 bay leaf

2 cloves of garlic

1 onion

1 tomato

Olive oil

Salt and pepper

eMPLOYMENT

Cut, arrange and fry the rabbit over high heat. Take out and reserve.

On low heat, fry the onion and garlic cut into small pieces in the same oil for 5 minutes. Increase the heat and add the chopped tomato. Boil until there is no water left.

Add the rabbit again and coat it with wine. Let it reduce and the sauce will be almost dry. Brush with stock and cook with aromatic herbs for 25 minutes or until meat is tender.

Meanwhile, fry the cleaned and laminated mushrooms in a hot pan for 2 minutes. Season with salt and add to the stew. Cook for another 2 minutes and adjust the amount of salt if necessary.

Lies

You can make the same recipe with chicken or turkey.

ESCALOPE MADRILEÑA

INGREDIENTS

4 beef fillets

1 tablespoon fresh parsley

2 cloves of garlic

Flour, eggs and breadcrumbs (for coating)

Olive oil

Salt and pepper

eMPLOYMENT

Finely chop the parsley and garlic. We put them in a bowl and add the bread crumbs. Remove.

We coat the fillet with salt and pepper and rub the mixture of flour, beaten eggs and bread with garlic and parsley.

Press down with your hands to make sure the patty sticks well and fry in plenty of very hot oil for 15 seconds.

Lies

Rub the tenderloin with a mallet to break the fibers and make the meat more tender.

GET RABBIT WITH MUSHROOMS

INGREDIENTS

1 rabbit

250 g of seasonal mushrooms

50 g of fat

200 g of ham

45 g of almonds

600 ml of chicken stock

1 glass of sherry

1 carrot

1 tomato

1 onion

1 clove of garlic

1 sprig of thyme

Salt and pepper

eMPLOYMENT

Wait for the rabbit season. Fry over high heat in butter together with the ham cut into sticks. Take out and reserve.

In the same fat, fry the onion, carrot and garlic cut into small pieces. Add the chopped mushrooms and cook for 2 minutes. Add the chopped tomatoes and cook until it loses its water.

Add back the rabbit and ham and deglaze with wine. Let it reduce and the sauce will be almost dry. Moisten with gravy and add thyme. Cook on low for 25 minutes or until the rabbit is tender. Sprinkle with almonds and season with salt.

Lies

You can use dried shiitake mushrooms. They add a lot of flavor and aroma.

IBERIAN PORK RIBS WITH WHITE WINE AND HONEY

INGREDIENTS

1 Iberian pork rib

1 glass of white wine

2 spoons of honey

1 tablespoon sweet paprika

1 tablespoon of chopped rosemary

1 tablespoon of minced thyme

1 clove of garlic

Olive oil

Salt and pepper

eMPLOYMENT

Add the spices, minced garlic, honey and salt to a bowl. Add ½ cup oil and mix. Brush the ribs with this mixture.

Bake at 200 degrees for 30 minutes, meat side down. Turn, baste with wine and cook for another 30 minutes or until the ribs are golden and tender.

Lies

In order for the flavors to absorb more in the ribs, it is better to marinate the meat the day before.

CHOCOLATE PEPPER PEARS

INGREDIENTS

150 g of chocolate

85 g of sugar

½ liter of milk

4 pears

1 cinnamon stick

10 peppers

eMPLOYMENT

Peel the pears without removing the stem. Boil in milk together with sugar, cinnamon stick and peppercorns for 20 minutes.

Remove the pears, strain the milk and add the chocolate. Let it reduce, stirring constantly, until it thickens. Serve the pears with the chocolate sauce.

Lies

When the pears are cooked, open them lengthwise, remove the core and cover them with mascarpone cheese and sugar. Close again and the season. Delicious.

THREE CHOCOLATE CAKES WITH BISCUITS

INGREDIENTS

150 g of white chocolate

150 g of dark chocolate

150 g of milk chocolate

450 ml of cream

450 ml of milk

4 tablespoons of butter

1 package of Maria cookies

3 packages of cottage cheese

eMPLOYMENT

Crush the biscuits and melt the butter. Crush the biscuits with butter and form the base of the cake in removable form. Leave it in the fridge for 20 minutes.

Meanwhile, heat 150 g of milk, 150 g of cream and 150 g of one of the chocolate desserts in a container. As soon as it starts to boil, dilute 1 package of cottage cheese in a glass with a little milk and pour the mixture into the jar. We take it out as soon as it is cooked again.

Place the first chocolate on the cookie dough and put it in the refrigerator for 20 minutes.

Repeat the same with the other chocolate and place it on top of the first layer. And repeat the operation with the third chocolate. Refrigerate or refrigerate until ready to serve.

Lies

You can also use other chocolates, such as mint or orange.

MARING Switzerland

INGREDIENTS

250 g of sugar

4 egg whites

a pinch of salt

A few drops of lemon juice

eMPLOYMENT

Beat the egg whites with a stick until stiff. Add lemon juice, a little salt and sugar little by little and without stopping to beat.

After adding the sugar, beat for another 3 minutes.

Lies

When the beaten egg whites are stiff, this is called peak point or snow point.

HAZELNUT CREAM WITH BANANAS

INGREDIENTS

100 g of flour

25 g of butter

25 g of sugar

1 ½ dl of milk

8 spoons of hazelnut cream

2 spoons of rum

1 spoon of powdered sugar

2 bananas

1 egg

½ packet of yeast

eMPLOYMENT

Beat the egg, yeast, rum, flour, sugar and milk. Let it rest in the refrigerator for 30 minutes.

Heat the butter in a non-stick pan over low heat and spread a thin layer of batter over the entire surface. Flip until it turns a light golden color.

Peel and cut the bananas. Spread 2 tablespoons of hazelnut cream and ½ banana on top of each pancake. Close the pastry and sprinkle with powdered sugar.

Lies

Crepes can be made in advance. When they are ready to eat, just heat them in a pan with a little butter on both sides.

LEMON CAKE WITH CHOCOLATE BASE

INGREDIENTS

400 ml of milk

300 g of sugar

250 g of flour

125 g of butter

50 g of cocoa

50 g of corn starch

5 yellow

Juice of 2 lemons

eMPLOYMENT

Mix flour, butter, 100 g of sugar and cocoa until you get the consistency of sand. Then add water until you get a dough that does not stick to your hands. Line the mold, pour this cream and bake at 170ºC for 20 minutes.

Or heat the milk. Meanwhile, beat the egg yolks and the remaining sugar until they pale slightly. Then add cornstarch and mix with milk. Heat stirring constantly until thickened. Add lemon juice and continue mixing.

Assemble the cake by filling the base with cream. Let it rest in the fridge for 3 hours before serving.

Lies

Add some mint leaves to the lemon frosting to give the cake the perfect freshness.

inquiry

INGREDIENTS

500 g of mascarpone cheese

120 g of sugar

1 package ladyfingers cookies

6 eggs

Amaretto (or aged rum)

1 large cup of coffee (sweetened to taste)

cocoa powder

Salt

eMPLOYMENT

Separate the whites and yolks. Add the yolks and add half the sugar and the mascarpone cheese. Hit with reeling moves and actions. Beat the egg whites to peaks (or snow) with a pinch of salt. When they are almost set, add the other half of the sugar and finish setting. Mix the yolks and whites in a gentle, rolling motion.

Dip the cookies in coffee and alcohol on both sides (without getting too wet) and place them at the bottom of the container.

Spread a layer of egg and cream cheese on top of the cookies. Wet the soletilla cookies again and place them on top of the dough. Finish with cheese mixture and sprinkle with cocoa powder.

Lies

Eat overnight or preferably two days after preparation.

INTXAURSALSA (walnut cream)

INGREDIENTS

125 g of shelled walnuts

100 g of sugar

1 liter of milk

1 small cinnamon stick

eMPLOYMENT

Boil milk with cinnamon and add sugar and chopped nuts.

Simmer for 2 hours and let cool before serving.

Lies

It should have the consistency of rice pudding.

MERINGUE MILK

INGREDIENTS

175 g of sugar

1 liter of milk

1 lemon peel

1 cinnamon stick

3 or 4 egg whites

Cinnamon powder

eMPLOYMENT

Heat the milk with the cinnamon stick and lemon zest over low heat until it starts to boil. Immediately add the sugar and cook for another 5 minutes. Reserve and let cool in the fridge.

When cool, beat the egg whites until stiff and pour in the milk. Serve with cinnamon powder.

Lies

For the final granita, place in the freezer and poke with a fork every hour until completely frozen.

LANGUAGES OF THE MASS

INGREDIENTS

350 g of loose flour

250 g butter pomade

250 g of powdered sugar

5 egg whites

1 egg

VANILLA

Salt

eMPLOYMENT

Put the butter, powdered sugar, a little salt and a little vanilla essence in a bowl. Beat well and add the egg. Continue beating and add the egg whites one at a time. Add the flour all at once without mixing it too much.

Put the cream in a piping bag with a smooth tip and make strips about 10 cm. Tap the plate on the counter to spread the batter and bake at 200ºC until the tops are golden.

Lies

Add 1 tablespoon of coconut powder to the batter to make different cat tongues.

ORANGE HATS

INGREDIENTS

220 g of flour

200 g of sugar

4 eggs

1 small orange

1 in chemical yeast

Cinnamon powder

220 g of sunflower oil

eMPLOYMENT

Mix the eggs with the sugar, cinnamon and orange zest and juice.

Add the oil and mix. Add the sifted flour and yeast. Let this mixture sit for 15 minutes and pour it into the cake pan.

Heat the oven to 200 degrees and bake them for 15 minutes until they are cooked.

Lies

You can add chocolate chips to the dough.

BAKED APPLE WITH PORT

INGREDIENTS

80 g of butter (in 4 pieces)

8 spoons of port wine

4 spoons of sugar

4 pippin apples

eMPLOYMENT

Spread the apples. Fill with sugar and put butter on top.

Bake for 30 minutes at 175ºC. After this time, sprinkle each apple with 2 tablespoons of port wine and bake for another 15 minutes.

Lies

Serve warm with a scoop of vanilla ice cream and drizzle with the juices.

COOKED MARINGO

INGREDIENTS

400 g granulated sugar

100 g of powdered sugar

¼ liter of egg white

drops of lemon juice

eMPLOYMENT

Beat the egg whites with the lemon juice and sugar in a bain marie until well combined. Remove from the heat and continue to mix (the meringue will thicken as it loses temperature).

Add powdered sugar and continue beating until the meringue is completely cooled.

Lies

It can be used to cover cakes and make decorations. The temperature is not higher than 60 ºC, so that the egg white does not harden.

KRAUTISHKA

INGREDIENTS

170 g of sugar

1 liter of milk

1 tablespoon of cornstarch

8 egg yolks

1 lemon peel

cinnamon

eMPLOYMENT

Boil the milk with the lemon peel and half the sugar. Once it boils, cover and let it rest from the heat.

In a separate bowl, beat the egg yolks with the remaining sugar and cornstarch. Add a quarter of the boiled milk and continue to mix.

Add the yolk mixture to the remaining milk and cook, stirring constantly.

After the first boil, beat them with a whip for 15 seconds. Remove from heat and continue to stir for another 30 seconds. Drain and let cool. Sprinkle with cinnamon.

Lies

To make a flavored cream - chocolate, crushed cookies, coffee, grated coconut, etc. - just remove it from the heat and mix it to the desired taste while it is hot.

KAMBLETA PEOPLE'S PANNA KOTA

INGREDIENTS

150 g of sugar

100 g purple candy

½ l of cream

½ liter of milk

9 sheets of gelatin

eMPLOYMENT

Wipe the gelatin sheets from the cold water.

Heat the cream, milk, sugar and candies in a pot until they melt.

Remove from heat, add gelatin and stir until completely dissolved.

Pour into molds and refrigerate for at least 5 hours.

Lies

You can change this recipe by mixing it with toffee, coffee, etc.

AGRICULTURAL BISCUITS

INGREDIENTS

220 g of soft butter

170 grams of flour

55 g of powdered sugar

35 g of corn starch

5 g of orange peel

5 g of lemon peel

2 tablespoons of orange juice

1 tablespoon of lemon juice

1 egg white

VANILLA

eMPLOYMENT

Very slowly mix together the butter, egg white, orange juice, lemon juice, citrus zest and a pinch of vanilla essence. Mix and add the sifted flour and cornstarch.

Place the dough in a piping bag and draw 7cm circles on the parchment paper. Bake for 15 minutes at 175ºC.

Sprinkle the cookies with powdered sugar.

Lies

Add ground cloves and ginger to the batter. The result is excellent.

MANGO PASTE

INGREDIENTS

550 g of loose flour

400 g of soft butter

200 g of powdered sugar

125 g of milk

2 eggs

VANILLA

Salt

eMPLOYMENT

Mix the flour, sugar, a pinch of salt and another vanilla essence. Beat in the not too cold eggs one at a time. Beat with a little warm milk and add the sifted flour.

Place the dough in a piping bag fitted with a curling tip and pipe a little onto the parchment paper. Bake at 180ºC for 10 min.

Lies

You can add crushed almonds, sprinkle with chocolate or stick cherries on the outside.

YOGURT CAKE

INGREDIENTS

375 g of flour

250 g of natural yogurt

250 g of sugar

1 packet of chemical yeast

5 eggs

1 small orange

1 lemon

125 g of sunflower oil

eMPLOYMENT

Beat the eggs and sugar with a mixer for 5 minutes. Mix with yogurt, oil, zest and citrus juice.

Sift flour and yeast and mix with yogurt.

Grease and flour the pan. We pour the dough and bake it at 165 ºC for about 35 minutes.

Lies

Use flavored yogurt to make a variety of cookies.

BANANA COMPOST ROSEMARY

INGREDIENTS

30 g of butter

1 sprig of rosemary

2 bananas

eMPLOYMENT

Peel and cut the bananas.

We put them in a pot, cover them and cook them on very low heat with butter and rosemary until the banana is like compote.

Lies

This compote is suitable for both pork chops and chocolate chip cookies. You can add 1 spoon of sugar during cooking to make it sweeter.

GARDEN

INGREDIENTS

100 g of brown sugar

100 g of white sugar

400 cl of cream

300 cl of milk

6 egg yolks

1 vanilla pod

eMPLOYMENT

Open the vanilla bean and extract the seeds.

In a bowl, beat the milk with white sugar, egg yolks, cream and vanilla. Fill individual molds with this mixture.

Heat the oven to 100 degrees and bake in a water bath for 90 minutes. When cool, sprinkle with brown sugar and torch (or preheat the oven to maximum grill mode and cook until the sugar burns slightly).

Lies

Add 1 tablespoon of instant cocoa to cream or milk for a delicious cocoa brûlée.

GYPSY HAND FOUNDED BY GRETIN

INGREDIENTS

250 g of chocolate

125 g of sugar

½ l of cream

Soletilla Cookies (see "Desserts" section)

eMPLOYMENT

Make a soletilla cookie. Fill with whipped cream and roll.

In a pot, boil the sugar together with 125 g of water. Add the chocolate, melt without stopping for 3 minutes and cover the roll with it. Let it rest before serving.

Lies

To enjoy an even more complete and delicious dessert, add small pieces of fruit with syrup to the cream.

FLANGE EGG

INGREDIENTS

200 g of sugar

1 liter of milk

8 eggs

eMPLOYMENT

Cook on low heat and without mixing the caramel with the sugar. When it turns brown, remove from heat. Split into individual panels or any shape.

Whisk in the milk and eggs to prevent foaming. If it appears before you put it in the molds, remove it completely.

Pour the caramel on top and bake at 165ºC for about 45 minutes or until a skewer inserted comes out clean.

Lies

The same recipe makes a delicious pudding. Just mix the croissants, buns, cookies left over from the day before into the mix.

JELLE CAVA WITH FLOWERS

INGREDIENTS

500 g of sugar

150 g of strawberries

1 bottle of cava

½ packet of gelatin sheets

eMPLOYMENT

Heat the cava and sugar in a saucepan. Remove the previously soaked gelatin in cold water from the heat.

Serve in strawberry martini glasses and refrigerate until set.

Lies

It can also be made with any sweet and red fruit wine.

FRIES

INGREDIENTS

150 grams of flour

30 g of butter

250 ml of milk

4 eggs

1 lemon

eMPLOYMENT

Boil the milk and butter together with the lemon zest. When it boils, remove the skin and immediately add the flour. Turn off the heat and stir for 30 seconds.

We put it back on the fire and mix it for another minute until the dough does not stick to the sides of the pan.

Put the dough in a container and add the eggs one by one (don't add the next one until the first one is well mixed with the dough).

With the help of a pastry bag or 2 spoons, fry the patties in small pieces

Lies

It can be filled with cream, cream, chocolate, etc.

SAN JUAN COCA

INGREDIENTS

350 g of flour

100 g of butter

40 g of pine nuts

250 ml of milk

1 packet of baking powder

1 lemon peel

3 eggs

sugar

Salt

eMPLOYMENT

Sift the flour and yeast. Mix and make a volcano. Put the skin, 110 g of sugar, butter, milk, eggs and a little salt in the center. Knead well until the dough does not stick to your hands.

Roll until it is rectangular and thin. Place on a plate lined with baking paper and leave to ferment for 30 minutes.

Brush with coconut egg, sprinkle with pine nuts and 1 tablespoon of sugar. Bake it at 200 ºC for about 25 min.

Bolognese sauce

INGREDIENTS

600 g of chopped tomatoes

500 g ground beef

1 glass of red wine

3 carrots

2 celery sticks (optional)

2 cloves of garlic

1 onion

oregano

sugar

Olive oil

Salt and pepper

eMPLOYMENT

Finely chop the onion, garlic, celery sticks and carrots. Grease it and when the vegetables are soft, add the meat.

Deglaze and deglaze with wine when the pink color of the meat disappears. Leave for 3 minutes on high heat.

Add the chopped tomatoes and simmer over low heat for 1 hour. At the end, adjust the salt and sugar and add oregano to taste.

Lies

Bolognese is always paired with pasta, but it's delicious with rice pilaf.

WHITE CHEESE (CHICKEN OR BEEF)

INGREDIENTS

1 kg beef or chicken bones

1 dl white wine

1 celery stick

1 sprig of thyme

2 cloves

1 bay leaf

1 clean pair

1 clean carrot

½ onion

15 black pepper

eMPLOYMENT

Put all the ingredients in a pot. Cover with water and cook on medium heat. When it starts to boil, skim it. Cook for 4 hours.

Strain through a chinois and transfer to another bowl. Store immediately in the refrigerator.

Lies

Do not salt it before use as it spoils more easily. It is used as a base in sauces, soups, rice dishes, stews, etc.

TOMATO CONSUL

INGREDIENTS

1 kg of tomatoes

120 g of onion

2 cloves of garlic

1 sprig of rosemary

1 sprig of thyme

sugar

1 dl olive oil

Salt

eMPLOYMENT

Cut the onion and garlic into small pieces. Simmer slowly in the pan for 10 minutes.

Chop the tomatoes and add them to the pan with the herbs. Cook until the tomatoes lose all their water.

Sprinkle with salt and add rectified sugar if necessary.

Lies

It can be prepared in advance and stored in an airtight container in the refrigerator.

ROBERT'S SAUCE

INGREDIENTS

200 g of onion

100 g of butter

½ l broth

¼ liter of white wine

1 tablespoon of flour

1 tablespoon of mustard

Salt and pepper

eMPLOYMENT

Fry the onion cut into small pieces in butter. Add the flour and cook slowly for 5 minutes.

Increase the heat, pour in the wine and let it reduce by half, stirring constantly.

Add the stock and cook for another 5 minutes. Remove from heat, mix with mustard and season with salt and pepper.

Lies

Ideal with pork.

PINK sauce

INGREDIENTS

250 g of mayonnaise sauce (see the section "Soups and sauces")

2 spoons of ketchup

2 spoons of brandy

½ orange juice

Tabasco

Salt and pepper

eMPLOYMENT

Mix mayonnaise, ketchup, brandy, stock, a pinch of tabasco, salt and pepper. Beat well until you get a homogeneous sauce.

Lies

To make the sauce smoother, add ½ tablespoon of mustard and 2 tablespoons of heavy cream.

FISH PROMOTION

INGREDIENTS

500 g bones or white fish heads

1 dl white wine

1 sprig of parsley

1 pair

½ small onion

5 peppercorns

eMPLOYMENT

Put all the ingredients in a pot and pour 1 liter of cold water. Cook on medium heat for 20 minutes without skimming.

Drain, transfer to another container and refrigerate quickly.

Lies

Do not salt it before use as it spoils more easily. This includes sauces, rice dishes, soups, etc.

GERMAN SAUCE

INGREDIENTS

35 g of butter

35 g of flour

2 egg yolks

½ l soup (fish, meat, poultry, etc.)

Salt

eMPLOYMENT

Fry the flour in the butter over low heat for 5 minutes. Immediately add the stock and cook over medium heat for another 15 minutes, stirring constantly. Adjust the salt.

Remove from the heat and add the yolks, stirring constantly.

Lies

Do not overheat so that the yolks do not curdle.

Bold sauce

INGREDIENTS

750 g of fried tomatoes

1 small glass of white wine

3 tablespoons of vinegar

10 raw almonds

10 chili peppers

5 slices of bread

3 cloves of garlic

1 onion

sugar

Olive oil

Salt

eMPLOYMENT

Fry all the garlic in a pan. Remove and reserve. Fry the almonds in the same oil. Remove and reserve. In the same pan, toast the bread. Remove and reserve.

In the same oil, fry the chopped onion together with the chili. When it is boiled, soak it with vinegar and a glass of wine. Leave for 3 minutes on high heat.

Add the tomato, garlic, almonds and bread. Cook for 5 minutes, stir and add salt and sugar if necessary.

Lies

It can be frozen in individual ice cube trays and used only as needed.

Dark Gravy (Chicken OR VIPI)

INGREDIENTS

5 kg beef or chicken bones

500 g of tomatoes

250 g of carrots

250 grams of leeks

125 g onion

½ liter of red wine

5 liters of cold water

1 sprig pio

3 bay leaves

2 sprigs of thyme

2 sprigs of rosemary

15 peppers

eMPLOYMENT

Bake the cubes at 185ºC until light brown. Put the cleaned and medium vegetables in the same pan. Allow the vegetables to brown.

Place the bones and vegetables in a large pot. Add wine and herbs, add water. Cook for 6 hours on low heat, skimming occasionally. Drain and let cool.

Lies

It is used in many sauces, stews, rice dishes, soups, etc. base. When the soup cools, the fat remains frozen on top. This makes removal easier.

PICON MOJO

INGREDIENTS

8 tablespoons of vinegar

2 teaspoons cumin seeds

2 teaspoons of paprika

2 heads of garlic

3 cayenne peppers

30 spoons of oil

coarse salt

eMPLOYMENT

Grind all the solid ingredients except the paprika in a mortar and pestle until you get a paste.

Add the paprika and continue to grind. Gradually add the liquids until you get a homogeneous and emulsified sauce.

Lies

Ideal with the famous crinkled potatoes, as well as grilled fish.

PESTO sauce

INGREDIENTS

100 g of pine nuts

100 grams of parmesan

1 bunch fresh basil

1 clove of garlic

mild olive oil

eMPLOYMENT

Grind all the ingredients without leaving it too homogeneous to notice the crunch of the pine nuts.

Lies

You can replace the walnuts with pine nuts and the basil with fresh arugula. At first, this is done with a mortar.

Sweet and sour sauce

INGREDIENTS

100 g of sugar

100 ml of vinegar

50 ml of soy sauce

1 lemon peel

1 orange peel

eMPLOYMENT

Boil the sugar, vinegar, soy sauce and citrus peel for 10 minutes. Allow to cool before use.

Lies

It's a great addition to spring rolls.

GREEN MOJITO

INGREDIENTS

8 tablespoons of vinegar

2 teaspoons cumin seeds

4 green pepper balls

2 heads of garlic

1 bunch parsley or cilantro

30 spoons of oil

coarse salt

eMPLOYMENT

Mix all the hard ingredients until you get a paste.

Gradually add the liquids until you get a homogeneous and emulsified sauce.

Lies

It can be stored covered in plastic wrap, chilled in the refrigerator for several days without any problems.

BESAMEL sauce

INGREDIENTS

85 g of butter

85 g of flour

1 liter of milk

Nutmeg

Salt and pepper

eMPLOYMENT

Melt the butter in a saucepan, add the flour and cook over low heat for 10 minutes, stirring constantly.

Pour the milk immediately and cook for another 20 minutes. Keep stirring. Season with salt, pepper and nutmeg.

Lies

To avoid lumps, cook the flour and butter over low heat, stirring constantly, until the mixture is almost liquid.

Hunter's Sauce

INGREDIENTS

200 g of mushrooms

200 g of tomato sauce

125 g of butter

½ l broth

¼ liter of white wine

1 tablespoon of flour

1 small onion

Salt and pepper

eMPLOYMENT

Fry the finely chopped onion in butter on medium heat for 5 minutes.

Add the cleaned and quartered mushrooms and increase the heat. Cook for another 5 minutes until the water is gone. Add the flour and cook for another 5 minutes, stirring constantly.

Deglaze with wine and allow to reduce. Add tomato sauce and broth. Cook another 5 minutes.

Lies

We leave it in the refrigerator and put a light film of butter on top so that a crust does not form on the surface.

AIOLI sauce

INGREDIENTS

6 cloves of garlic

vinegar

½ l light olive oil

Salt

eMPLOYMENT

Crush the garlic with salt in a press and mortar until you get a paste.

Add the oil little by little, mixing it continuously with a pestle and mortar, until you get a thick sauce. Add a splash of vinegar to the sauce.

Lies

If 1 egg yolk is added while grinding the garlic, the sauce becomes lighter.

AMERICAN sauce

INGREDIENTS

150 g of lobster

250 g of shrimp and shrimp and prawn heads

250 g of ripe tomatoes

250 g of onion

100 g of butter

50 g of carrots

50 grams of leeks

½ l fish stock

1 dl white wine

½ dl brandy

1 tablespoon of flour

Level 1 teaspoon of chili pepper

1 sprig of thyme

Salt

eMPLOYMENT

Fry the vegetables, except the tomatoes, in small pieces in butter. Then fry the pepper and flour.

Fry the remaining crabs and crustacean heads and deglaze with brandy. Reserve the crab tails and grind the carcasses with smoke. Drain 2 or 3 times until no skins remain.

Add the smoke, wine, quartered tomatoes and thyme to the vegetables. Boil for 40 minutes, mash and mash with salt.

Lies

A wonderful sauce for stuffed peppers, monkfish or fish pie.

Dawn Sauce

INGREDIENTS

45 g of butter

½ l velouté sauce (see "Soups and sauces" section)

3 spoons of tomato sauce

eMPLOYMENT

Boil the Velute sauce, add a spoonful of tomatoes and beat with a whisk.

Remove from the heat, add the butter and continue to mix until well combined.

Lies

Use this sauce on some poached eggs.

BARBECUE SAUCE

INGREDIENTS

1 can of coke

1 cup tomato sauce

1 cup ketchup

½ glass of vinegar

1 teaspoon of oregano

1 teaspoon of thyme

1 teaspoon cumin

1 clove of garlic

1 ground cayenne

½ onion

Olive oil

Salt and pepper

eMPLOYMENT

Cut the onion and garlic into small pieces and fry in a little oil. When it is soft, add tomatoes, ketchup and vinegar.

Cook for 3 min. Add cayenne and spices. Stir, add Coca-Cola and cook until a thick texture remains.

Lies

This is a great dip for chicken wings. It can be frozen in individual ice cube trays and used only as needed.

BEARNAISE SAUCE

INGREDIENTS

250 g of clarified butter

1 dl tarragon vinegar

1 dl white wine

3 egg yolks

1 onion (or ½ small onion)

Tarragon

Salt and pepper

eMPLOYMENT

Heat the shallots cut into small pieces in a saucepan together with the vinegar and wine. Let it reduce until you have about 1 tbsp.

Place the salted yolks in a bain-marie. Add the wine vinegar reduction and 2 tablespoons cold water until doubled in volume.

While continuing to beat, gradually pour the melted butter into the yolks. Add some crushed tarragon and keep in a water bath at a temperature not higher than 50ºC.

Lies

It's important to keep this sauce in a bain-marie over low heat so it doesn't boil.

Carbonated sauce

INGREDIENTS

200 g of ham

200 g of cream

150 grams of parmesan

1 medium onion

3 egg yolks

Salt and pepper

eMPLOYMENT

Fry the onion cut into small cubes. When it is fried, add the ham cut into thin strips and leave it on the fire until it turns golden.

Then add the cream, season with salt and pepper and cook slowly for 20 minutes.

Remove from the heat, add the grated cheese, the yolks and mix.

Lies

If you have leftovers for another occasion, after heating, do it on low heat and not too long so that the egg does not curdle.

CHARCUTERA sauce

INGREDIENTS

200 g of onion

100 g pickled cucumbers

100 g of butter

½ l broth

125 cl of white wine

125 cl of vinegar

1 tablespoon of mustard

1 tablespoon of flour

Salt and pepper

eMPLOYMENT

Fry the chopped onion in butter. Add the flour and cook slowly for 5 minutes.

Increase the heat and pour in the wine, vinegar and let it reduce by half, stirring constantly.

Pour the juice, pickles and cook another 5 minutes. Remove from the heat and add the mustard. The season.

Lies

This sauce is ideal for fatty meat.

CUMBERLAND SAUCE

INGREDIENTS

150 g of blackcurrant jam

½ dl port

1 cup dark broth (see Gravy and Sauces section)

1 teaspoon of powdered ginger

1 tablespoon of mustard

1 onion

½ orange peel

½ lemon peel

½ orange juice

½ lemon juice

Salt and pepper

eMPLOYMENT

Finely grate the orange and lemon peels. Boil in cold water and boil for 10 seconds. Repeat the operation 2 times. Drain and cool.

Finely chop the shallots and cook for 1 minute, stirring constantly, with the red grape jam, port, stock, citrus zest and juice, mustard, ginger, salt and pepper. Let it cool.

Lies

It is an excellent sauce for pates or game dishes.

KURRI sauce

INGREDIENTS

200 g of onion

2 spoons of flour

2 tablespoons of curry

3 cloves of garlic

2 large tomatoes

1 sprig of thyme

1 bay leaf

1 bottle of coconut milk

1 apple

1 banana

Olive oil

Salt

eMPLOYMENT

Fry the garlic and onion cut into small pieces in oil. Add the curry and fry for 3 minutes. Add the flour and cook for another 5 minutes, stirring constantly.

Add the quartered tomatoes, herbs and coconut milk. Cook for 30 minutes on low heat. Add the peeled and diced apple and banana and cook for another 5 minutes. Crush the salt, filter and correct.

Lies

To make this sauce lower in calories, cut the amount of coconut milk in half and replace it with chicken stock.

Garlic sauce

INGREDIENTS

250 ml of cream

10 cloves of garlic

Salt and pepper

eMPLOYMENT

Blanch the garlic 3 times in cold water. Boil, drain and boil again with cold water. Repeat this action 3 times.

When it bubbles, cook for 25 minutes together with the cream. At the end, adjust them with salt and pepper.

Lies

Not all creams are created equal. If it is too thick, add a little cream and cook for another 5 minutes. On the other hand, if it is too runny, cook it longer. Perfect with fish.

Grape sauce

INGREDIENTS

200 g of berries

25 g of sugar

250 ml Spanish sauce (see "Soups and sauces" section)

100 ml of sweet wine

2 tablespoons of vinegar

1 tablespoon of butter

Salt and pepper

eMPLOYMENT

Make sugar caramel over low heat. Add the vinegar, wine, berries and cook for 15 minutes.

Pour in the Spanish sauce. Adjust them with salt and pepper, mix them, filter them and boil them together with butter.

Lies

This is a great game sauce.

Cider sauce

INGREDIENTS

250 ml of cream

1 bottle of cider

1 zucchini

1 carrot

1 pair

Salt

eMPLOYMENT

Cut the vegetables into cubes and boil for 3 minutes on high heat. Pour the cider and leave for 5 minutes.

Add the cream, salt and cook for another 15 minutes.

Lies

A great accompaniment to a grilled mushroom or a piece of salmon.

Ketchup

INGREDIENTS

1 ½ kg of ripe tomatoes

250 g of onion

1 glass of white wine

1 ham bone

2 cloves of garlic

1 large carrot

fresh thyme

fresh rosemary

Sugar (optional)

Salt

eMPLOYMENT

Cut the onion, garlic and carrot into julienne strips and fry over medium heat. When the vegetables have softened, add the bone and pour the wine. Raise the fire.

Add the quartered tomatoes and herbs. Cook for 30 minutes.

Remove the bones and herbs. Cut, filter and remove salt and sugar if necessary.

Lies

Freeze in individual ice cube trays to always have delicious homemade tomato sauce on hand.

PEDRO XIMENEZ wine sauce

INGREDIENTS

35 g of butter

250 ml Spanish sauce (see "Soups and sauces" section)

75 ml Pedro Ximénez wine

Salt and pepper

eMPLOYMENT

Heat the wine for 5 minutes over medium heat. Add the Spanish sauce and cook for another 5 minutes.

To thicken and make it glossy, take off the heat and add the cold cubed butter. The season.

Lies

It can be made with any sweet wine, such as

Cream sauce

INGREDIENTS

½ l béchamel sauce (see section "Soups and sauces")

200 cl of cream

½ lemon juice

eMPLOYMENT

Boil the béchamel and pour the cream. Cook until you have about 400 cl of sauce.

Remove from heat and add lemon juice.

Lies

Ideal for sauce au gratin, fish and poached eggs.

Mayonnaise sauce

INGREDIENTS

2 eggs

½ lemon juice

½ l light olive oil

Salt and pepper

eMPLOYMENT

Add the eggs and lemon juice to a mixing glass.

Beat with a blender 5 gradually adding the oil without stopping. Season with salt and pepper.

Lies

Add 1 tablespoon of hot water to the blender jar with the rest of the ingredients to prevent tearing.

YOGURT AND SUSCE CAP

INGREDIENTS

20 g of onion

75 ml mayonnaise sauce (see the "Soups and sauces" section)

1 tablespoon of honey

2 yogurts

Dill

Salt

eMPLOYMENT

Mix all the ingredients, except the dill, until you get a smooth sauce.

Finely chop the dill and add to the sauce. Remove and correct the salt.

Lies

Perfect with chips or lamb.

Devil's Sauce

INGREDIENTS

100 g of butter

½ l broth

3 dl white wine

1 small onion

2 peppers

Salt

eMPLOYMENT

Cut the onion into small pieces and fry at a high temperature. Add the chilli, pour in the wine and let it reduce by half.

Brush with meat broth, cook for another 5 minutes and add salt and spices.

Add the very cold butter off the heat and beat with a whisk until thick and glossy.

Lies

This sauce can also be made with sweet wine. The result is extraordinary.

SPANISH SAUCE

INGREDIENTS

30 g of butter

30 g of flour

1 l broth (reduced)

Salt and pepper

eMPLOYMENT

Fry the flour in the butter until it gets a slightly browned shade.

Pour in the boiled liquid, stirring constantly. Cook for 5 minutes and season with salt and pepper.

Lies

This sauce is the basis of many preparations. This is what is called a basic sauce in the kitchen.

Hollandaise sauce

INGREDIENTS

250 g of butter

3 egg yolks

¼ lemon juice

Salt and pepper

eMPLOYMENT

Melt the butter.

Place the yolks in a bain-marie along with a pinch of salt, pepper and lemon juice and 2 tablespoons of cold water until doubled in volume.

While continuing to beat, gradually pour the melted butter into the yolks. Keep the water bath at a temperature not higher than 50 ºC.

Lies

This sauce is amazing on small baked potatoes with smoked salmon on top.

ITALIAN CLOTHES

INGREDIENTS

125 g of tomato sauce

100 g of mushrooms

50 g York ham

50 g of onion

45 g of butter

125ml Spanish sauce (see Sauces and Sauces section)

90 ml of white wine

1 sprig of thyme

1 sprig of rosemary

Salt and pepper

eMPLOYMENT

Finely chop the onion and fry in butter. When they soften, increase the heat and add the sliced and cleaned mushrooms. Add the diced ham.

Add the wine and herbs and allow to reduce completely.

Add the Spanish sauce and tomato sauce. Cook for 10 minutes, add salt and pepper.

Lies

Perfect for pasta and boiled eggs.

Mousse sauce

INGREDIENTS

250 g of butter

85 ml of whipping cream

3 egg yolks

¼ lemon juice

Salt and pepper

eMPLOYMENT

Melt the butter.

Put the yolks in a bain-marie along with some salt, pepper and lemon juice. Add 2 tablespoons cold water until doubled in volume. While continuing to beat, gradually add the butter to the yolks.

Right at the moment of serving, beat the cream and pour it into the previous mixture with soft and enveloping movements.

Lies

Keep the water bath at a temperature not higher than 50 ºC. Perfect for seasoning salmon, razor clams, asparagus, etc.

RIMOULED sauce

INGREDIENTS

250 g of mayonnaise sauce (see the section "Soups and sauces")

50 g pickled cucumbers

50 g of capers

10 g of anchovies

1 teaspoon chopped fresh parsley

eMPLOYMENT

Grind the anchovies in a press and mortar until thick. Cut capers and pickles into very small pieces. Add the rest of the ingredients and mix.

Lies

Perfect for some deviled eggs.

BIZCAINE SAUCE

INGREDIENTS

500 g of onion

400 g of fresh tomatoes

25 g of bread

3 cloves of garlic

4 chorizo or ñora peppers

Sugar (optional)

Olive oil

Salt

eMPLOYMENT

Drain the ñoras to remove the flesh.

Sauté the onions and garlic over medium heat in a covered pan for 25 minutes.

Add the bread and diced tomatoes and continue baking for another 10 minutes. Add the ñor meat and cook for another 10 minutes.

Puree and adjust salt and sugar if necessary.

Lies

Although unusual, this is a wonderful sauce to use with spaghetti.

Red sauce

INGREDIENTS

2 cloves of garlic

1 large tomato

1 small onion

½ small red pepper

½ small green pepper

2 bags of squid ink

White wine

Olive oil

Salt

eMPLOYMENT

Cut the vegetables into small pieces and simmer slowly for 30 minutes.

Add the chopped tomatoes and cook over medium heat until the water evaporates. Increase the heat and add the ink bags and a splash of wine. Let it reduce by half.

Mix, filter and season with salt.

Lies

Adding a little more ink after grinding will make the sauce brighter.

BREAKFAST SAUCE

INGREDIENTS

75 g Parmesan cheese

75 g of butter

75 g of flour

1 liter of milk

2 egg yolks

Nutmeg

Salt and pepper

eMPLOYMENT

Melt the butter in a saucepan. Add the flour and cook over low heat for 10 minutes, stirring constantly.

Pour in the milk at once and cook for another 20 minutes, stirring constantly.

Add the egg yolks and cheese from the heat and continue to mix. Season with salt, pepper and nutmeg.

Lies

This is the perfect gratin sauce. Any type of cheese can be used.

ROMESCO sauce

INGREDIENTS

100 g of vinegar

80 g of roasted almonds

½ teaspoon sweet paprika

2 or 3 ripe tomatoes

2 peppers

1 small slice of toast

1 head of garlic

1 chili pepper

250 g of extra virgin olive oil

Salt

eMPLOYMENT

Boil the ñoras in hot water for 30 minutes. Remove the pulp and reserve.

Heat the oven to 200 degrees and roast the tomatoes and a head of garlic (tomatoes need about 15 or 20 minutes, and garlic a little less).

After roasting, clean the skin and seeds of the tomatoes, remove the garlic one by one. Place in a blender along with the almonds, toast, ñora meat, oil and vinegar. Beat well.

Then add the sweet pepper and a pinch of chili pepper. Beat again and adjust the salt.

Lies

Do not over mix the sauce.

SOUBISE sauce

INGREDIENTS

100 g of butter

85 g of flour

1 liter of milk

1 onion

Nutmeg

Salt and pepper

eMPLOYMENT

Melt the butter in a saucepan and slowly fry the onion cut into thin strips for 25 minutes. Add the flour and cook for another 10 minutes, stirring constantly

Pour the milk immediately and cook for another 20 minutes on low heat, stirring constantly. Season with salt, pepper and nutmeg.

Lies

It can be served as it is or pureed. Perfect with cannelloni.

TARTAR SAUCE

INGREDIENTS

250 g of mayonnaise sauce (see the section "Soups and sauces")

20 g of onion

1 tablespoon capers

1 tablespoon fresh parsley

1 tablespoon of mustard

1 pickled cucumber

1 hard-boiled egg

Salt

eMPLOYMENT

Finely chop the onion, capers, parsley, pickled cucumber and boiled egg.

Mix everything and add mayonnaise and mustard. Add a pinch of salt.

Lies

It is an excellent accompaniment to fish and cold meat.

Irish dressing

INGREDIENTS

150 g of sugar

70 g of butter

300 ml of cream

eMPLOYMENT

Caramelize the butter and sugar without mixing at any time.

When the caramel turns brown, remove from the heat and add the cream. Cook for 2 minutes on high heat.

Lies

Iris can be flavored by adding 1 sprig of rosemary.

VEGETABLE SOUP

INGREDIENTS

250 g of carrots

250 grams of leeks

250 g of tomatoes

150 g of onion

150 g of turnips

100 g of celery

Salt

eMPLOYMENT

Wash the vegetables well and cut them into regular pieces. Place in a pot and cover with cold water.

Cook on low heat for 2 hours. Drain and season with salt.

Lies

A good cream can be made from the vegetables used. Always cook uncovered to allow the flavors to better concentrate as the water evaporates.

www.ingramcontent.com/pod-product-compliance
Lightning Source LLC
Chambersburg PA
CBHW050159130526
44591CB00034B/1396